BBC MUSIC GUIDES

SCHOENBERG CHAMBER MUSIC

28th Sept.

Ar. 29th Sept.

BBC MUSIC GUIDES

General Editor: GERALD ABRAHAM

BBC MUSIC GUIDES

Schoenberg Chamber Music

ARNOLD WHITTALL

BRITISH BROADCASTING CORPORATION

List of works discussed

Music example no. 1(a) is reproduced by kind permission of Faber Music Ltd, London; nos. 1(b), 2–6, 8, 10–12 of Universal Edition (Alfred A. Kalmus Ltd.); no. 7 of Wilhelm Hansen, Musik-Forlag, Copenhagen; nos. 13–15 of G. Schirmer, 140 Strand, London; no. 16 of Boelke and Bomart, New York; no. 17 © 1952 by C. P. Peters Corporation, New York. The extracts from Schoenberg's *Letters* are by kind permission of Faber and Faber Ltd and St Martin's Press, Inc.

Published by the British Broadcasting Corporation
35 Marylebone High Street, London W1M 4AA
ISBN 0 563 10489 9
First published 1972
© Arnold Whittall 1972
Printed in England by The Whitefriars Press Ltd,
London and Tonbridge

1897 - 1906

I may say that for the present it matters more to me if people understand my older works . . . . They are the natural forerunners of my later works, and only those who understand and comprehend them will be able to hear the latter with any understanding beyond the fashionable minimum. And only such people will realise that the melodic character of these later works is the natural consequence of my earlier experiments . . . . I do not attach so much importance to being a musical bogy-man as to being a natural continuer of properly understood good old tradition! [Letter 73][1]

Arnold Schoenberg was forty-eight when, in July 1923, he wrote the letter to Werner Reinhart which includes this statement of belief, a statement all the more significant because it was made at the time when he was beginning to use his own recently developed method of twelve-note composition. Now that musical pace-making is in the hands of composers like Stockhausen, it is increasingly easy to hear the truth of Schoenberg's claim. Indeed the obviously traditional aspects of form and texture present in his twelve-note, or serial, music are the very elements which some dislike intensely, believing as they do that serialism should from the very beginning have made a more decisive break with the past. On the other hand, those who continue to regard tonality as essential to any valid form of composition feel that Schoenberg ceased to communicate in music as soon as he abandoned tonality, and his attempt to combine atonal serialism with classical musical structures is seen as futile and unpleasant.

Most of the important central figures of modern music have, at one time or another, been too radical for some, too conservative for others, and twenty or more years after his death the same is still true of Schoenberg. My object is therefore to examine his chamber music in a way which may help the listener to recognise, if not to admire, the relationship between conservative and radical elements in the music itself. This will entail discussion of four basic questions: How did he use tonality? Why did he abandon it? How did he organise atonality? Why, in his serial works, did he retain forms developed during the years when tonality was central to all music?

Schoenberg's chamber music is particularly suitable as material

[1] All letters referred to by number are from Arnold Schoenberg, *Letters,* selected and edited by Erwin Stein, translated by Eithne Wilkins and Ernst Kaiser (London 1964).

or the discussion of these questions. Starting with the D major String Quartet of 1897 and ending with the Phantasy for violin with piano accompaniment of 1949, there is a regular succession of works for a wide variety of instrumental combinations, illustrating every stage of his development. It may often seem as if the discussion of these works as chamber music takes second place to a discussion of more general technical matters, but this is inevitable, especially with music where the medium – string quartet or wind quintet, for example – may be the most conventional, traditional feature; every effort has been made to make technicalities both relevant and comprehensible.

Schoenberg himself said that he was educated primarily by playing and writing chamber music, and his early musical life – he was born in Vienna in 1874 – led him, in particular, to the medium of the string quartet. Although he was essentially self-taught as a composer, it is nonsense to infer that even in youth he was an embryonic anarchist, so narcissistic that his interest in any music earlier than his own was of the slightest. The opposite is true. Perhaps it was precisely because he was never subjected to the worst sorts of academic constraints that Schoenberg's devotion to musical tradition was so profound. And what could be more logical than to wish to pay Mahler and Brahms, the most recent inheritors of that tradition, the honour, not of slavish imitation, but of building on their achievements – learning from them, but not simply copying them?

Schoenberg started composing before the age of nine, and his technique developed as his violin playing developed. From the very start he wrote music to play himself, with friends or relations. The urge to compose string quartets, however, came when he bought some Beethoven scores, including two of the Op. 59 Razumovskys and the *Grosse Fuge*. His friend Oscar Adler gave him some basic information about harmony, though this may have been little more than Schoenberg had already deduced from his study of the music itself. Similarly, at the age of about eighteen he discovered the 'rules' of sonata form in a recently published encyclopedia, Meyer's *Konversationslexicon* – doubtless an interesting experience for someone already deeply immersed in the great works of the classical tradition.

During the mid-1890s Schoenberg wrote five or six string quartets, profiting from discussion with composition students at the Vienna Conservatoire and with his close friend Alexander von Zemlinsky. The last of these apprentice works, dating from 1897 though not published until 1966, is the first to survive: a Quartet in D major which fully exhibits the talents of the young composer. No one would claim that it is a work of great originality. It is, however, full of confidence and spontaneity, the obvious influences of Dvořák, Brahms and Smetana acting not simply as evidence of Schoenberg's familiarity with relatively recent works by established masters, but as the foundation of an ambitious, large-scale structure.

The four movements are in the keys of D major, F sharp minor, B flat minor and D major, a tonal scheme which divides the scale symmetrically into major thirds in a manner reminiscent of the later Beethoven (for example, the *Hammerklavier* Sonata). It also leads naturally to a concept of expanded tonality, bringing keys (other than close relatives like dominant and relative minor) into an immediate yet logical relationship with the basic key of the whole work. Such a concept of expansion could also be applied to the relationships between chords and types of chords, and although the early quartet is still essentially conventional in its harmonic reliance on triads and sevenths, Schoenberg was soon to carry his explorations into this field also.

In the first movement of the Quartet Schoenberg uses as his main alternative tonal centres B major and F major, which are also symmetrically related to D as minor thirds above and below. A major, the dominant, is shunned in the first movement, but becomes the subsidiary key of the short Intermezzo, where it is likewise in a mediant relationship to F sharp minor. After a set of variations which remains close to B flat minor throughout, the rondo finale ranges widely in tonality, using conventional relatives (for example, the dominant minor) as well as the more distant regions (B and F) established in the first movement.

Schoenberg exploits harmonic relationships in this Quartet in such a way as to create a balance between the flat and sharp areas of the tonal system. It is this balance which makes the ultimate confrontation, in the finale, between E flat, B flat and D logical as well as exciting. To the more intellectual kind of late-romantic composer it may well have seemed that one of the weaknesses of earlier tonal schemes was the way in which one area of the whole (flat or sharp) tended to dominate the other: and the more chromaticism was emphasised, the more wide-ranging modulations were used, the more it became essential to preserve some sense of hierarchy – of a central tonic with other keys ranged around it in varying degrees of importance – by the employment of logical, symmetrical patterns of the kind used by Schoenberg here.

There are many striking points of detail in the work, enhancing the strong overall conception. The use of a three-note stepwise ascent starting from the tonic in several themes is a unifying factor which may well be intentional. There is also a characteristically bold use of thematic inversion at the start of the first movement's 'development',[1] one of many examples of a conscious emphasis on contrapuntal device. Moreover, even within the triadic language of the work there are a good many adventurous but effective harmonic progressions.

As Egon Wellesz tells us, Schoenberg was invariably harsh with young composers who rushed into print. He would ask 'if they could not have waited till they had written something mature, there being no necessity to publish things that showed good intentions but insufficient mastery of form'.[2] If mastery of form were the only criterion of maturity, the 1897 Quartet is undoubtedly mature. But Schoenberg must also have attached importance to style, to a clear expression of the composer's own personality, and in this respect the early work, for all its skill and confidence, is still a student piece. It was also Schoenberg's first important work to achieve public performance, but the fact that it was well received did not prevent what he described as

an almost sudden turn towards a more 'progressive' manner of composing . . . . Mahler and Strauss had appeared on the musical scene, and so fascinating was their advent that every musician was immediately forced to take sides, pro or contra. Being then only twenty-three years of age, I was easily to catch fire, and to begin composing symphonic poems of one uninterrupted movement, the size of the models given by Mahler and Strauss.[3]

Such preoccupations might have been expected to turn Schoenberg away from chamber music to large orchestral forces. Nevertheless, the impact of Mahler and Strauss did not deprive him of all capacity for individual thought, and his first extant symphonic

[1] Schoenberg preferred the German word *Durchführung*, meaning elaboration.

[2] Wellesz, *Arnold Schoenberg* (London 1925), p. 59.

[3] U. Rauchhaupt (ed.), *Schoenberg, Berg and Webern. The String Quartets: A documentary study* (Hamburg 1971), p. 36.

poem was also, surprisingly, a piece of chamber music, scored for string sextet.

Verklärte Nacht, after a poem by Richard Dehmel, was composed in a mere three weeks in September 1899. Centred like the early Quartet on a tonality of D, it is Schoenberg's first fully mature achievement. Certainly its musical language is more comprehensive than that of the Quartet, the relatively untroubled diatonicism of the latter yielding to a rich mixture of diatonic and chromatic elements. Along with harmony, texture and structure are more ambitious, more individual, far from the Brahms-Strauss hybrid which a simple description of the literary subject-matter and the instrumentation might suggest.

The structure of *Verklärte Nacht* is determined by the five stanzas of Dehmel's poem. This describes a woman confessing to a man that she is to bear a child not his, and the man's acceptance and forgiveness. The statements of the woman and the man (sections two and four) are framed by short stanzas which depict the setting through which they walk, a bare, cold wood at night. In the final stanza the menace of their surroundings has dissolved, just as the sombre D minor of Schoenberg's opening is transformed into the radiant D major of the ending.

Verklärte Nacht may owe something to both Brahms and Strauss, but by far the largest debt is to Wagner, and that in spite of the happy ending, which makes the work a *Liebesleben* rather than, as is sometimes claimed, a kind of *Liebestod*, after *Tristan und Isolde*. Schoenberg said that he learned from Wagner 'the possibility of transforming the expressive qualities of themes, and the right way to construct them for this purpose'.[1] Since the Wagnerian *Leitmotiv* seemed to Schoenberg to provide the means whereby the diverse thematic material necessary for an entire opera could be unified by relationships with one fundamental theme, it is not surprising that he eventually saw a similarity of purpose between this concept of *Leitmotiv* and his own basic set in twelve-note music, from which all pitches, thematic, ornamental and accompanimental, were derived. And twenty years before the emergence of the concept of the basic set, Schoenberg demonstrated, in *Verklärte Nacht,* his concern for 'developing variation', whereby new thematic elements grow organically from a basic idea.

[1] Joseph Rufer, *The Works of Arnold Schoenberg*, translated by Dika Newlin (London 1962), p. 147.

According to Schoenberg, Wagner's greatest weakness was his excessive use of sequences and semi-sequences. *Verklärte Nacht* contains a certain amount of sequential repetition, as well as the more developmental variants which, Schoenberg claimed, were Brahmsian rather than Wagnerian in origin. Yet the true Wagnerian essence of *Verklärte Nacht* lies in Schoenberg's instinctive grasp of dynamic inter-relationships between large musical paragraphs (a grasp soon to be still more impressively displayed in the gigantic *Gurrelieder*) whereby those various kinds of repetition, exact or evolutionary, are given large-scale cohesion by careful control and direction of their harmonic implications, both with regard to their immediate context and to their position in the work as a whole.

Like the 1897 Quartet, *Verklärte Nacht* avoids the closest relative keys of its tonic D, preferring instead more remote alternatives like E major, B flat minor, F sharp major and D flat major. When, in the early stages of the work, the tonality moves away from the initial D minor, it tends to 'float' rather than to establish clear alternatives, and Schoenberg's sequential treatment of chromatic material obviously increases tonal instability as well as structurally expanding the paragraph in question. The dramatic manipulation of tonal expectation is well illustrated at an early climax point (*Lebhaft bewegt,* p. 15) where an implied return to the D minor tonic provokes instead a long, agitated, virtually atonal outburst. A little later on, near the end of the second section, a return to the tonic is again prepared (*Sehr langsam,* p. 22) and again deflected. When D (major) is finally established at the centre of the work (at the beginning of the fourth section, p. 26), it is merely the starting point for a new cycle involving modulation and expansion, a cycle in which one dominant preparation in the tonic (p. 38) is side-stepped before the final enriched return (pp. 41–2).

Verklärte Nacht is a music-drama without words in which powerful contrasts of texture and tonality are balanced by subtle thematic inter-relationships and by a highly concentrated contrapuntal complexity. Even if some of the simpler triadic moments in the work sound sententious, they are as vital a complement to the dissonant polyphony as the man's lack of vindictiveness is to the woman's sense of guilt. The language and the atmosphere of the poem itself may have dated, but the urgency and nobility of the music are still vivid and convincing.

Egon Wellesz[1] feels that a greater expressive intensity is achieved if the work is played by more than one performer to a part, and since Schoenberg himself made two arrangements of the work for string orchestra (1917 and 1943 respectively), he too must have regarded the richer sonorities as a valid alternative, even if there is a corresponding loss of intimacy and refinement.

Verklärte Nacht marked the beginning of Schoenberg's long struggle for the performance of his music: 'it sounds as if someone had smeared the score of *Tristan* while it was still wet' was the comment of one member of a 'jury' which examined its suitability for performance at the Tonkünstlerverein in Vienna. Yet the 'single uncatalogued dissonance' (X in Ex. 1*b*), which led to the initial rejection of the work in Vienna, is, in context, simply an intensification of the kind of dramatic chromatic emphasis which is found, for example, at the end of the development section in the first movement of the 1897 Quartet:

Ex. 1
(a) 1897 Quartet

(b) Verklärte Nacht

[1] *Op. cit.,* p. 67.

It is clear now, as Ex. 1 shows, that Schoenberg's 'emancipation of the dissonance' was indissolubly associated with the expansion of tonality. In Ex. 1 (b), quite clearly, the chromatic chords do not lead to a new key – they are not potentially diatonic: they colour the existing key. Yet what to us is vividly expressive was, to late nineteenth-century conservatives, extravagantly disruptive. On the threshold of the twentieth century Schoenberg seemed to them to be parting company with the present, and writing music which only an unimaginable future would take to its heart and revere.

The third of Schoenberg's D-centred chamber works is the String Quartet No. 1, Op. 7, finished on 26 September 1905 and first performed by the Rosé Quartet on 5 February 1907 after some forty rehearsals. Many years later, in his essay 'Heart and Brain in Music', Schoenberg recalled how, on morning walks, 'I composed in my mind forty to eighty measures [of Op. 7] complete in almost every detail. I needed only two or three hours to copy down these large sections from memory.' Schoenberg's claim that even a fast writer could not copy such passages in less time than it took him to create them may be naïvely boastful, but it emphasises the tremendous fluency with which he normally composed. As he later wrote in an essay:

A composer must not compose two or eight or sixteen measures today and again tomorrow and so on until the work seems to be finished, but should conceive a composition as a totality, in one single act of inspiration. Intoxicated by his idea, he should write down as much as he could [*sic*], not caring for little details. They could be added, or carried out later.

Verklärte Nacht was, as we said, written in three weeks, and contains 415 bars. Yet Schoenberg claimed to have worked for a whole hour on one single bar (at letter H) of particular contrapuntal complexity. There may be similar bars in Op. 7, but the whole work gives the impression of having been conceived in one tremendous burst of inspiration. In the composer's own words on another subject, it 'is so homogeneous in its composition that in every little detail it reveals its truest, inmost essence'. In the scope of its single-movement form, the quality of its thematic material, the lucidity of its chromatic-diatonic, dissonant-consonant, contrapuntal-homophonic relationships, this masterpiece shows Schoenberg's genius at full stretch, his rethinking of traditional functions at its most imaginative.

There were more nineteenth-century precedents for running the three or four traditionally separate movements of a sonata or symphony together to make one continuous movement than there were for expanding single sonata-form movements by introducing elements of slow movement or scherzo between sections. Apart from *Verklärte Nacht*, Schoenberg had already composed a large-scale, single-movement orchestral symphonic poem, *Pelleas und Melisande,* Op. 5 (1902–3), which is close in dimensions to Strauss's *Ein Heldenleben,* though remote in subject and atmosphere. Just as, near the end of Schoenberg's life, a new stage in his development is represented by the one-movement String Trio and Violin Phantasy so, between 1904 and 1906, crucial events concerning the concentration of musical form and the modification of functional tonality occur in the Quartet, Op. 7, and its immediate successor, the First Chamber Symphony, Op. 9, which are both single-movement compositions.

'Concentrated' may seem precisely the wrong word to apply to a single, 45-minute movement. Indeed, by the side of Op. 9, Op. 7 seems expansive. By the side of other important contemporary works – for example, Mahler's gigantic Sixth Symphony – its concentration is manifest, especially as it exploits relatively few of the expectations which the listener instinctively experiences in tonal music. Schoenberg himself made clear that 'the great expansion of this work required a careful organisation' and stressed how much he owed to a study of the first movement of Beethoven's *Eroica* Symphony.[1]

The most remarkable thing about the D minor Quartet, and the most difficult to elucidate verbally, is its sense of proportion on two interacting levels. First, there is the level of exposition. Schoenberg presents his thematic material in groups appropriate in character to the traditional genres of fast first movement, scherzo, slow movement and rondo finale. The work is in no sense monothematic: a composition on such a scale needs strong thematic contrast. Tonality, not theme, is the essential unifying factor.

The areas of exposition are linked, anticipated, and, more importantly, transformed by large areas of development, areas which form the second structural level of the work. It is in these developments that Schoenberg's 'lucid complexity' is at its most

[1] Cf. Schoenberg's own note on the work in Rauchhaupt, *op. cit.,* p. 39.

breath-taking. Thematic variation and combination, though protean in their manifestations, remain perfectly under control. Most important of all, however, is the fact that the dynamism of the developments, by making themes from different expositions compatible, renders any large-scale separate recapitulation unnecessary and, indeed, impossible. The potentialities of the material are fully utilised in development, and so the rondo 'finale' section introduces no new main themes but concentrates instead on further discussion of material from all three areas of exposition. The most important return in the work – at letter O – is to the initial tonal centre of D – minor at the outset, major in the coda. Closing the tonal circle is satisfying intellectually: it is also, like the passage at letter W of *Verklärte Nacht* which it resembles, intensely poignant, the final transformation of the first theme of the work in the cello preparing a cadence prolonged by anguished chromaticisms and ultimately completed by three richly-spaced D major triads.

Alban Berg once wrote an essay with the rather despairing title 'Why is Schoenberg's music so difficult to understand?', in which he illustrated how, from the very first bar, the D minor Quartet modifies expected procedures of phrase structure and harmonic relationship. Hans Keller has declared that in Op. 7 'atonality is rife – even though the key-signature is D minor'.[1] These atonal passages fit, even though they lack the functional progressions, the accepted procedures of the tonal passages, simply because music weak in 'function' is strong in direction. It still progresses, but its tensions and relaxations are more rhythmic or textural than, in the traditional sense, harmonic.

Already, in this work, we can discern the 'key' to Schoenberg's view of atonality. All through the nineteenth century, dissonances had gradually been freed from their original function of preparing, and resolving on to, concords. They now existed, in their own right, as higher consonances. But Schoenberg did not believe that, with the abandonment of tonal progression, the textures and structures built on phrase-succession and cadential effect should also be abandoned. Atonality would provide the justification for retaining these traditional elements of musical phraseology, rather than implying their elimination.

In other words, Schoenberg came to regard tonality as only one of the elements of traditional composition. Form and texture,

[1] 'Schoenberg as Music', *The Listener*, 7 January 1965, p. 34.

tension and relaxation, could operate either in terms of tonality or independently of it. Hence the fact that there is no conflict between the atonal and tonal passages of the D minor Quartet, even though occasional progressions, notably the cadences at letter G (Ex. 2) and at 13 and 14 bars after letter L, seem ugly because of the rather crude way in which the chromaticism is introduced:

Fluency and expansiveness are indeed the keynotes of this work, whether with regard to rhythm (Schoenberg is often accused of being excessively four-square, but that he could be the reverse of this where appropriate is clear, for example, on page 76); instrumental effects (even if the 'sul ponticello' passages do not substantially enhance the musical atmosphere); or, inevitably, in the choice of main alternative tonalities – G flat and F – always bearing in mind that in Op. 7 the real alternative to the basic D is *a*tonality.

As far as is known, no one ever asked Schoenberg if he considered it illogical to reject one aspect of tradition while preserving others. But the answer given by his later music is clear. Tonality was exhausted, as the result of natural, evolutionary forces present in its own constitution. The forms hitherto associated with it but not inseparable from it – and, to some extent, even the triads which had been its main harmonic element – were not exhausted. In brief – harmonic logic and drama, coupled with thematic argument, were the essential ingredients of a valid musical form. And harmony may function logically without tonality.

In outline, the First Chamber Symphony, Op. 9, completed on 25 July 1906 (just ten months after Op. 7), has a similar structure to the Quartet: a first section exposing two main thematic groups and some development; a scherzo; a central development section, ending with emphatic recollections of the opening material (though not, in Op. 9, in the tonic key); a slower section with new thematic ideas; and a 'finale' or recapitulation section which is more a second development in its fundamental concern with discovering new relationships between versions of themes from earlier sections (the second development of Op. 7 is more demo-cratic than that of Op. 9, where no scherzo material appears).

The Chamber Symphony is only half as long as the D minor Quartet, and appropriately its basic tempo direction is *Sehr rasch* (very fast), as opposed to the *Nicht zu rasch* (not too fast) which replaced the original *Sehr lebhaft* (very lively) at the head of the Quartet. Nevertheless, it is worth noting here that the main complaint in Schoenberg's letter to the conductor Hermann Scherchen (11 February 1914) is that his tempi in the Chamber Symphony were too fast throughout (Letter 21). Since greater speed is matched by greater density – the work is scored for fifteen solo instruments – problems of balance are considerable, and there are times when the texture can sound congested. It must be almost impossible to balance five strings and ten winds, parti-cularly when the latter group includes a bass clarinet and a double bassoon. Egon Wellesz, referring to early performances of the work, notes that in large halls it was found necessary to increase the number of strings, and that such an increase greatly assisted the listener's understanding of the music.[1] Stravinsky, for one, was never attracted by the sound of the solo strings – 'they remind me of the economy-sized movie-theatre orchestras of the 1920s – though I agree that the multiple-string version tames and blunts the piece unduly'.[2] When performed with multiple strings, of course, the Symphony ceases to be chamber music, if the fact that it needs a conductor even in its original version has not already deprived it of this status.

As in the D minor Quartet, thematic contrast is as crucial to the design of the work as tonal unity. In his essay 'Composition with Twelve Tones', Schoenberg describes how, after completing the Chamber Symphony, he was worried by the apparent absence of any relationship between the two principal themes of the first section. He restrained his inclination to replace the second theme, and, about twenty years later, was rewarded by perceiving the 'true' relationship:

[1] Cf. Wellesz, *op. cit.,* p. 104.
[2] Igor Stravinsky and Robert Craft, *Dialogues and a Diary* (London 1968), p. 106.

Ex. 3

Schoenberg firmly believed that 'in music there is no form without logic, there is no logic without unity'. Yet he was far from claiming that the creation of unity was any more a cerebral process than the act of composition itself. On one occasion he referred to composition as 'slowed-down improvisation; often one cannot write fast enough to keep up with the stream of ideas'. And elsewhere he referred to 'inspirations which come only to the genius, who receives them unconsciously and formulates solutions without noticing that a problem has confronted him'.

Clearly the unity between Schoenberg's two themes was created subconsciously. Unfortunately the composer does not tell us whether *all* the themes of the First Chamber Symphony are unified in this way. How, for example, can one relate the slow section theme to the 'basic motive'? It may be possible to do so, but its function is surely primarily one of contrast within the tonal and harmonic unity of the work as a whole. The fact is that motivic or thematic unity is not a necessary, inevitable function of pre-twelve-note composition. If themes 'belong together' it is because of the way their contrasts and similarities are deployed within a particular harmonic and tonal framework. So, as far as the Chamber Symphony is concerned, it is true that important ideas from first and second subject groups share the interval of the perfect fourth, and that this interval is of great harmonic importance at certain points in the work as an 'irritant' to diatonicism. It is also true that another first subject group idea anticipates the slow section theme, but the contrast between these two ideas, at least on the surface, is unmistakable.

Even the faster sections of the work are relatively undiatonic and untriadic, so much so that a conventional cadence, like that which heralds the slow section, can sound disconcertingly banal. The return to E major at the end is achieved by progressions which affirm the tonic triad but little else which is diatonic to E major. Whole-tone approaches to the tonic triad are preferred. Anthony Payne has stressed that the chromatic, contrapuntal nature of much of the development in the Chamber Symphony deprives it of one basic attribute of traditional developments, that of 'a firm progress through strongly defined key areas'.[1] Yet, as with the D minor Quartet, progress as such there still is – progress by means of divorcing elements of rhythm, texture and phrase structure from traditional harmony, and using this harmony only as a basic, unifying factor which is often in the background. The dynamic excitement of the music, the product of Schoenberg's contrapuntal dexterity, ensures that even those listeners who can recognise the difference between tonal clarity and virtual atonality rarely, if ever, feel that the music has lost its way when it is 'in between' points of tonal affirmation.

As a note on the work shows, Schoenberg himself was well aware of the direction indicated by the First Chamber Symphony, a work in which the amount of unvaried repetition and of harmonic, accompanimental 'filling-in' is much less even than in the D minor Quartet. The effect of concentrating exclusively on one-movement forms had been to increase still further the nineteenth-century emphasis on development as the most dynamic aspect of sonata form, and on counterpoint as the most dynamic means of articulating an increasingly chromatic language.

We have one piece of evidence which could indicate that Schoenberg himself was not satisfied with the actual sound of Op. 9. In the Second Chamber Symphony, begun soon after the First though not finally completed until 1939, he uses more conventionally balanced forces, supporting a wind group of two flutes, two oboes (the second doubling English horn), two clarinets, two bassoons, two horns and two trumpets with a normal body of orchestral strings. The music is fascinating, but the title is surely a misnomer. It is best considered alongside Schoenberg's other works for full orchestra.

[1] *Schoenberg* (London 1966), p. 12.

1907 - 1912

In his essay 'On revient toujours' (1948) Schoenberg wrote:

When I had finished my first Kammersymphonie, Op. 9, I told my friends: 'Now I have established my style. I know now how I have to compose.' But my next work showed a great deviation from this style: it was a first step towards my present style . . . .

The work in question, the Second String Quartet, Op. 10, was begun on 9 March 1907 and finished on 11 July 1908. It represents, to a certain extent, a point of repose after the hectic, even at times neo-Straussian, atmosphere of Op. 9: above all, for all its innovations, it is unmistakably a piece of chamber music, in spirit as well as in style. Since he reverted here to four separate (though inevitably related) movements, Schoenberg was able to demonstrate that the concept of recapitulation could still mean more than a purely tonal return supporting even greater developmental activity. In the Second Quartet there is a different emphasis. Virtuosity of thematic manipulation may now be taken for granted. What is new, at least in the finale, is a further move from relative tonal stability at 'anchor points' to a much less decisive tonic emphasis. The coda of the D minor Quartet, in its diatonic warmth, balances and even neutralises the local atonality of large portions of the work. The final section of the Chamber Symphony prepares and reinforces the central E major triad while remaining sceptical about its diatonic relatives – a process which in itself is merely an extension of that post-Beethovenian unwillingness to stress close relatives of the main tonic key at the expense of more distant ones which was observable as early as the 1897 String Quartet. In the finale of the Second Quartet, the central F sharp triad just preserves its primacy: the movement is still in expanded tonality but it is of the most tenuous kind. It is Schoenberg's farewell to triadic tonal centres until he was again able to view them in the 1930s and 1940s as, on occasion, a valid alternative to atonal serialism.

As the composer himself wrote of the Second Quartet:

The key is presented distinctly at all the main dividing points of the formal organisation. Yet the overwhelming multitude of dissonances cannot be counterbalanced any longer by occasional returns to such tonal triads as represent a key. It seemed inadequate to force a movement into the Procrustean bed of a tonality without supporting it by harmonic progressions that pertain to it.[1]

[1] 'My evolution', *Musical Quarterly*, XXXVII, 1952, pp. 522-3.

On another occasion, Schoenberg commented as follows on this crucial phase of his development:

The transition from composition which still emphasised key (while always containing many dissonances) to one where there is no longer any key, any tonic, any consonances, happened gradually, in accordance not with any wish or will, but with a *vision*, an *inspiration*; it happened perhaps instinctively.[1]

The sonata-form first movement of the Second Quartet is as subtle as it might have been had Schoenberg composed full, separate sonata-form movements in each of his previous works. A basic F sharp minor tonality functions, though conventional diatonic progressions are rare. From both the structural and harmonic viewpoints the movement is endlessly fascinating, though it will prove endlessly irritating to those who prefer inflexible statements of 'fact' to a discussion of possibilities.

Schoenberg's exposition is built on cunningly contrived ambiguities, so skilful that one forgets that this is a master manipulating a form which in lesser hands had already outlived its meaningfulness; it is almost possible to believe that one is witnessing the birth of a new, still flexible concept of musical form. At the climax of the lyric first subject the introductory motive reappears and leads to a passage (bars 43–9) which is more like a varied re-exposition of the first subject than a second group in the classical sense, particularly in the way it complicates, rather than changes, the main tonality. Even when a new motive appears (second violin, bar 50) it is initially combined with derivatives of the first theme (cello, bar 51).

Ex. 4

Only here, when the ear is getting used to the idea of development, does the first subject disappear, and, apart from the briefest of hints, the remaining thirty-two bars of the exposition unfold

[1] Quoted in Willi Reich, *Schoenberg*, translated by Leo Black (London 1971), p. 241.

independently of it, both motivically and tonally (when F sharp is absent from this movement, no clear alternative takes its place). It is a passing cadence in F sharp (bars 79–80) – *not* in a close relative, as would be the case in a classical movement – which signals the approaching end of the exposition, and emphasises the role of the tonic, not as a stimulus to modulation but rather as a refuge from a situation of no key at all.

Considering the exposition in isolation from the rest of the movement, however, the motive in bar 70 (first violin) might claim to be the 'real' second subject. If it is, it is neither developed nor recapitulated. Its function in the movement as a whole is to provide contrast, not simply of a thematic kind, but of a procedural kind. It stands back, rhetorically, from the developmental processes which occupy the rest of the movement.

The central development section starts in bar 90 with the introductory idea and proceeds to explore contrapuntal, canonic potentialities of both the first subject and the second subject counter-melody. At the end of this development (cf. bar 150), this counter-melody is grafted neatly on to the introductory idea, and preparations begin for the altered perfect cadence on F sharp which leads into the recapitulation at bar 159. In his own notes, Schoenberg seems to imply that the recapitulation begins in bar 146, with the return of what I have called the introductory idea in F – a curious suggestion in view of the strong *ritardando* leading to the return of the tonic key in bar 159.

In this final section all reference to the second subject motive is postponed until the coda (bar 218), a section in which the departures from and returns to the F sharp chord are as appealing emotionally as they are effective structurally. Not the least surprising and attractive thing about this movement, in view of the initial sections of the D minor Quartet and the First Chamber Symphony, is its strong lyric quality, a lyricism which flows and occasionally boils up into concentrated drama, but which at times has an almost elegiac atmosphere not unlike that of the first movement of the Second Chamber Symphony, on which Schoenberg had recently been working.

As has already been suggested, in the first three movements of Op. 10 the tonal centres are undermined not so much by modulation as by anti-tonal chromaticism, or, to use Schoenberg's own term – a useful one which has never caught on – pantonality.

The finale reverses the harmonic processes of the earlier movements to the extent that triads of F sharp gradually emerge from an initial atonality, thus dramatising the ultimate primacy of tonality in the whole work. The overall centrality of F sharp is also supported by the fact that both the middle movements use the alternative submediants of F sharp, D and D sharp ('spelt' as E flat) as tonal centres.

The second movement scherzo has twenty ₵ bars of exposition (three motives), 65 bars of development, centred for the most part on D, and a 13-bar recapitulatory coda. The trio, centred in D major, is faster and shorter – three sections, of 25, 28 and 14 bars respectively. A delicious transition incorporates both a reference to the Viennese street-song 'Ach du lieber Augustin' and a hint of the first movement material later to be developed in the third movement. The recapitulation of the scherzo is, inevitably, a second development, and is extended to 64 bars. A 17-bar coda is concerned solely with the first theme of the movement.

This scherzo is not particularly 'light', but it does demonstrate one aspect of Schoenberg's musical personality which is easily overlooked when discussion concentrates on his intellectual power – that is, the element of fantasy, of invention all the more exuberant for being disciplined. At times, indeed, it is not inappropriate to invert Schumann's comment on Chopin and describe Schoenberg's music as 'flowers buried in guns'. As for the use of Ach du lieber Augustin', with its claim that 'alles ist hin!' (all is lost): this lends support to the probability, hinted at by Schoenberg himself, that he was experiencing a particularly severe psychological crisis at the time. He might conceivably have felt at times that if 'all was lost' as far as tonality was concerned then he was also lost as a composer.

There is undoubtedly a conflict of a kind in Schoenberg between the sort of inspired instinctiveness which enabled him to compose so rapidly and the intellectual involvement, naturally most noticeable in the twelve-note works, where he takes a conscious pride in painstaking manipulation of the basic material. Perhaps serialism was so satisfying to Schoenberg simply because, in a way, it enabled him to take unity for granted, to develop flights of fancy without the possibility which, as we have seen, he feared for twenty years in the two main themes of the first section of the

First Chamber Symphony, that ideas which he *instinctively* felt to have a common origin might not actually have one.

The third movement of the Second Quartet is a set of five variations and a coda on a theme built out of four motives taken from the first and second movements. It is also a vocal movement, a setting of Stefan George's anguished poem 'Litanei' (Prayer). The music is almost totally thematic: only a few accompanimental figures are not clearly related to the main motives. In spite of the absence of conventional progressions, however, the harmonies still function, in the sense that they create tensions and relaxations relative to the basic E flat minor triad. For example, the instrumental coda resolves on to the tonic chord, creating a sense of cadence and finality none the weaker for not being 'orthodox':

Ex. 5

In his own note on this movement Schoenberg commented that he was

afraid the great dramatic emotionality of the poem might cause me to surpass the borderline of what should be admitted in chamber music. I expected the serious elaboration required by variation would keep me from becoming too dramatic.[1]

The form was also a means of continuing the process of development 'restricted or omitted' in the first two movements.

The sonata-form finale is also a vocal movement. Many commentators have eagerly seized on the 'air from other planets' mentioned in the first line of George's poem 'Entrückung' (Withdrawal) and it is indeed a convenient symbol of Schoenberg's

[1] Cf. Rauchhaupt, *op. cit.*, p. 47.

imminent 'lift-off' from tonality. The flickering figures of the introduction anticipate the atonal motivic material of the first Piano Piece, Op. 11, written soon after, but – as already suggested – the movement as a whole, in the context of the work as a whole, is notable for projecting little sense of a conflict between tendencies to abandon tonality on the one hand and preserve it on the other. The use of an F sharp major triad as a tonal focus – first of all at the end of the first vocal phrase or first subject statement (bar 25); then in the second subject (bars 52–65); at the start of the recapitulation (bar 100); and during the coda (bars 120–56) – is sufficiently frequent to enable one to hear the predominant chromaticism in terms of that ultimate tonic. What Schoenberg composed, therefore, was a sonata-form movement in expanded tonality, and any attempt to view it as a kind of 'Waterloo of Tonality' misses the point. There was no battle, no sudden renunciation of tradition. What Schoenberg carried over from the finale of Op. 10 into his post-tonal music was the traditional concept of musical material taking its character and identity from its actual pitch, whether that material be tonal or atonal; and the equally traditional concept that forms like sonata-form were still the best vehicles for the presentation of such material. As for the Second Quartet, this is not music in which Schoenberg was struggling against atonality, or fighting to save some vestige of key: it is that rarest of achievements, a transitional masterpiece, which does not demand to be heard in terms of its historical context but only in terms of its own beauty and strength.

In his essay 'New Music, Outmoded Music, Style and Idea', Schoenberg wrote:

Every tone which is added to a beginning tone makes the meaning of that tone doubtful . . . . In this manner there is produced a state of unrest, of imbalance which grows throughout the piece, and is enforced further by similar functions of rhythm. The method by which balance is restored seems to me the real *idea* of the composition.

This idea and a deep regard for traditional music – a profound understanding of which gave rise to the idea – remained with Schoenberg through all the upheavals and problems which now confronted him.

In December 1908 I attended one of the regular subscription concerts of the Rosé Quartet. They belonged to Vienna's musical events and took place in the dignified Bösendorfer Saal . . . . On the programme was a new string quartet in F sharp minor, by a young composer whose earlier works had already angered the Viennese . . . . This time matters were to become much worse. Already during the first two movements unrest was growing among the audience and some people left the hall. And hell broke loose when during an exposed passage a well-known critic got to his feet and shouted at the top of his voice: 'Stop it! Stop it! We have had enough!' It was then that people forgot their drawing-room manners: part of the audience joined in the riot which others tried to silence. There is a soprano solo in the last two movements which was sung by the great artist Marie Gutheil-Schoder. She and the Rosés did not lose their nerve and bravely carried the Quartet to its end, but not much of the music penetrated the noise.[1]

Erwin Stein's description of the first performance of the Second Quartet graphically illustrates the attitude of contemporary audiences to Schoenberg's work. Nevertheless, in spite of the hostility and the resulting difficulty of making a living as a teacher, the year 1909 was a remarkable one in Schoenberg's development. In it he completed the song cycle *Das Buch der Hängenden Gärten*, and composed the three Piano Pieces, Op. 11, the five Orchestral Pieces, Op. 16, and the 'monodrama' *Erwartung*, Op. 17. In these works he began to explore the world of atonality, and there was nothing in the least tentative about that exploration. Only in one respect – the feverish pace at which all of them, and especially *Erwartung*, were composed – is there evidence almost of reluctance to let the intellect interfere with the instinctive processes which could give birth to so much radically new music in so short a space of time. There is a sense of exhilaration in the fact that the technical mastery so prominent in the tonal works has not deserted the composer here. However, one result of this creative outburst was to carry Schoenberg's music not merely into the world of atonality but also, temporarily, into the world of 'athematicism'.

In both Op. 11 and Op. 16 it is possible to analyse much of the music in terms of particular motives which, in some cases, tend to recur at their initial pitch, functioning in a manner analogous to the themes of a tonal composition. In Op. 16, also, Schoenberg employed for the first time the terms 'Hauptstimme' (leading voice) and 'Nebenstimme' (subordinate voice) as a means of bringing clarity and hierarchy to the involved contrapuntal textures of the music. In *Erwartung*, however, it is almost impossible to isolate specific motives, whether the texture is dense or sparse, and although analysts have pored over the score, applying

[1] Erwin Stein, *Orpheus in New Guises* (London 1953), p. 48. Other accounts will be found in Rauchhaupt, *op. cit.*, pp. 141–7.

various sophisticated techniques to the music, they have up till now been forced to conclude that *Erwartung* presents an extreme example of music which, though possessing a high degree of consistency and continuity, does not depend for its effect on the regular recurrence of recognisable thematic elements in the way that almost all Schoenberg's other compositions do.

The loss of thematic identity as a result of the abandonment of tonality seems, in retrospect, a classic case of the baby and the bath water, and it is possible that only at this stage did the full extent of the problem of organising atonal music strike Schoenberg. Lecturing in 1941, he claimed that 'it seemed at first impossible to compose pieces of complicated organisation or of great length'. Perhaps he also meant that when conservative instincts were temporarily submerged by radicalism it seemed impossible to balance intellect and inspiration in the way the tonal Schoenberg had done and the serial Schoenberg would do again.

Certainly the reaction against the initial flood of atonal music was considerable. In 1910 Schoenberg completed nothing apart from the three pieces for chamber orchestra, which are of an extreme brevity more characteristic of his pupil Anton Webern. In 1911 this untypical involvement with the miniature continued in the Six Little Piano Pieces, Op. 19, and the tiny vocal piece *Herzgewächse*, Op. 20. True, he worked on the orchestration of the mammoth *Gurrelieder,* the composition of which was actually completed in 1901, but this activity itself indicates a need for respite as far as new projects were concerned.

Herzgewächse, one of the least compromising of all his works, is a setting in German translation of a poem by Maeterlinck. Written for soprano, celesta, harmonium and harp, it was first published in the German arts almanac *Der Blaue Reiter* in 1912. The extreme range of the vocal part, ascending at one point to F *in alt.,* makes that of the Second Quartet seem positively restricted, while the instrumentation, appropriate to the delicate, floral symbolism of the poem, is hardly an encouragement to frequent performance. In its avoidance of easily identifiable thematic elements, the music relates to that of *Erwartung.* However, it may not be too fanciful to deduce from the relatively calm atmosphere of the work that at least one crisis was over. In his next composition Schoenberg was to return to a more motivic type of working, enabling him once again to give clearer meaning to the concept of developing variation which he felt to be crucial in traditional music and still meaningful for modern composers. In this sense, the reference to formlessness in the first stanza of Maeterlinck's poem is apt:

'Neath the azure crystal bell
Of my listless melancholy
All my formless sorrows slowly
Sink to rest, and all is well.

A sense of disorder and chaos can be as effectively created in music by the use of simple effects and carefully organised technical devices as it can by a parallel avoidance of order and logic. Modern composers have tended to distinguish between the confusion of the insane and the obsessional symptoms of their madness – none more effectively than Berg in his opera *Wozzeck*. But in all cases it is recognised that madness is not so much an absence of logic as a replacement of 'real' logic by 'mad' logic.

The musical language of Schoenberg's *Pierrot Lunaire,* Op. 21, accepts this premise, the artificial ethos of texts in which extreme emotional states are expressed in simple verse-forms with a strong element of repetition (lines one and two recur as lines seven and eight, and the final, thirteenth line of each poem is a repetition of the first). The work was composed largely between 12 March and 30 May 1912 – proof of rediscovered fluency - and was written at the request of Albertine Zehme, who, as an actress not a singer, suggested that it should be a series of melodramas rather than a song cycle.

Fourteen of the twenty-one settings were written in one day each, and only two, nos. 14 and 15, were completed later, on 6 June and 9 July 1912 respectively. This fluency is important, for Schoenberg himself wrote many years later that the work was conceived in a 'light, ironical, satirical tone'[1]: and yet its impact, mainly because of the incantatory *Sprechgesang* or speech-song of the vocal line, is often mysterious rather than ironical, frightening rather than satirical.

The central theme of Giraud's 'three times seven' poems, which Schoenberg set in German translations by Otto Erich Hartleben, may indeed be a 'portrait of the artist', but it would have been extraordinary if the normally serious-minded Schoenberg, who later that same year was to embark on the text of an

[1] Rufer, *op. cit.,* p. 40.

oratorio, *Die Jakobsleiter,* concerned with modern man finding God and learning to pray, had ever regarded *Pierrot Lunaire* as anything other than a satire, though of a peculiarly savage kind. He even expressed surprise, in a letter of 1922, that movements like 'Madonna', 'Rote Messe' (Red Mass) and 'Die Kreuze' (The Crosses) should give religious offence:

Such a possibility never before crossed my mind and nothing was ever further from me in all my life than any such intention, since I have never at any time in my life been anti-religious, indeed I have never really been un-religious either. I seem to have had an altogether much naiver view of these poems than most people have and am still not quite uncertain that this is entirely unjustified [*sic*]. Anyway I am not responsible for what people make up their minds to read into the words. If they were musical, not a single one of them would give a damn for the words. Instead, they would go away whistling the tunes. But as it is, the modern musical public understands at best the WORDS, while for the rest it remains completely deaf to the music – on that point no amount of success in the world can delude me. [Letter 56]

Although it may seem unwise to proceed with a discussion of the poems after quoting that characteristic outburst, it is at least important to point out that the view, inferable from much of the text of *Pierrot Lunaire,* of the Clown-Artist as disoriented and disturbed is not necessarily an exact reflection of Schoenberg's own feelings about his treatment and position at this time. Nor does the work necessarily 'mean' that the artist can only find himself through madness, or any other such extremist idea. If anything, it represents a stage in that process of inner exploration which ultimately implied for Schoenberg acceptance of religious faith as the only way of escaping from that self-defeating absorption which is the result of unremitting introspection.

Since the nature of the vocal sound is so vital a part of the work's atmosphere – more so, indeed, than the 'tunes' – it is important to establish as clearly as possible what sound Schoenberg actually wanted. Rhythm and duration must, he says, be observed as exactly as they would be in a conventional, sung vocal line. Intervals and pitch are, by contrast, relative, while only the few notes so notated by Schoenberg must be sung at the exact pitch indicated. Hans Keller has pointed out a contradiction here:

His [Schoenberg's] instructions demand relative pitch; his notation implies absolute pitch – which indeed emerges incontrovertibly in the passacaglia and, in fact, in all the numbers where the speaking voice, at least intermittently, is written in strict counterpoint.[1]

[1] 'Whose Fault is the Speaking Voice', *Tempo 75,* 1966, p. 16.

Keller concludes that the contradiction was inevitable:

the instructions are written in the spirit of liberation – the liberation of the human voice; the notation springs from Schoenberg's instinctive need for reintegration. As a result, many performances which don't heed his instructions sound better than some which do . . .

Even if Schoenberg's instructions are contradictory, the question remains, why did he want the poems declaimed in this way? Perhaps we should look no further than the talents of Mme Zehme, and regard the contradictions as a practical solution to an insoluble problem. Yet it seems probable that, like all creative geniuses confronted with a problem not of their own making, Schoenberg accepted the challenge as an opportunity for experiment. Clearly he sought to create a closer relationship between speech and music than is possible in the ordinary melodrama, where the voice part may be notated only rhythmically. He also sought a more equally balanced relationship between the attributes of speech and music than is provided by song. And yet the effect is undeniably of song repressed, of the primitive and sophisticated, the impotent and fertile, in conflict. Such a conflict, between song and 'pre-song', with new symbolic associations, recurs in the opera *Moses und Aron,* where the sense of frustration, of inability to communicate, is a vital part of Moses' character. Pierrot, too, is talking to the moon; only when he is able to sing, it seems, will other human beings understand and want to listen.

Stravinsky has described *Pierrot Lunaire* as the 'solar plexus as well as the mind of early twentieth-century music'.[1] Although many musicians would prefer to apply this encomium to Stravinsky's own ballet *Le Sacre du Printemps,* it is undeniable that *Pierrot Lunaire,* mannerist rather than expressionist in its synthesis of order and disorder, is crucial to Schoenberg's development. In it he finally abandoned the tendency to asymmetrical, non-repetitive forms which he had explored in *Erwartung* and the Little Piano Pieces. Yet the work is still a long way from a return to the well-nigh total thematicism of the third movement of the Second Quartet or the first of the Op. 11 Piano Pieces. Only the specifically contrapuntal movements like 'Die Nacht' (a passacaglia) and 'Der Mondfleck' (a blend of fugue and canon) show such tendencies, and other movements still shun the exclusive exploitation of traditional forms which was to be one of the salient features of

[1] Stravinsky and Craft, *op. cit.,* p. 105.

the early twelve-note works of a decade later. A movement like 'Valse de Chopin' clearly shows the composer establishing some kind of an harmonic hierarchy simply by emphasis on a particular chord – another technique familiar from the Op. 11 Piano Pieces. Yet it is in the rhythmic patterns and phrase structure of *Pierrot Lunaire* that we can discern the decisive reacceptance of traditional musical periods, a reacceptance which grew from Schoenberg's decision to reflect, in his settings, the regular pulse and simple syntax of the verse itself.

Pierrot Lunaire is scored for a mixed quintet of instruments: piano, flute (doubling piccolo), clarinet (doubling bass clarinet), violin (doubling viola) and cello. Each of the twenty-one sections uses a different permutation of the available instruments, and the composer seizes every opportunity which the text provides for illustrative and atmospheric effects, often of an ironic kind, as in 'Serenade', when Pierrot's performance on the viola is the occasion for a virtuoso display on the *cello* (Ex. 6).

Much of the character of the work stems from the fact that, against its three-times-seven symmetrical substructure, the sequence of moods (and of instrumental combinations) is as unpredictable as the recurring moon-images are obsessive. Pure melodrama is exaggeration – of the rhythmic precision of speech, and of the differences of pitch in the normal rise and fall of speech. Yet the music does not exaggerate: it simply establishes the appropriate mood. This is the key to the disturbing world of *Pierrot Lunaire*. *Sprechgesang* is not in itself an exaggeration – it is the most appropriate way of presenting the extreme emotions of the text.

Pierrot is another of Schoenberg's chamber works to need a conductor. The first performance was given on 16 October 1912 in Berlin after more than forty rehearsals, with Mme Zehme in the costume of Columbine in front of dark screens behind which the musicians played, under Schoenberg's direction. Most of the audience were so enthusiastic that sections of the work had to be repeated, and although critics were divided on the accuracy of Mme Zehme's performance – as they have been about most subsequent interpreters of the work – it is clear that her commitment to the part was total and compelling. For once, therefore, Schoenberg had a success with a new work, though significantly it was in Berlin, not Vienna.

1923 - 1927

When Schoenberg composed *Pierrot Lunaire* he was living in Berlin, having moved there from Vienna in the autumn of 1911. In June 1912 he actually declined a post at the Vienna Academy – a post he had himself solicited two years before.

At this time he was much involved with performances of his own music. He conducted *Pierrot Lunaire* in various German and Austrian cities, often to the accompaniment of public disapproval. Following the first, and highly successful, performance of the

Gurrelieder in Vienna in 1913, conducted by Franz Schreker.
Schoenberg directed the work the following year in Leipzig, and
also performed the Five Orchestral Pieces, Op. 16, in Amsterdam
and London. After the outbreak of war he returned to Vienna
and was conscripted, though his age and health kept him well
away from the front. He was finally discharged on medical grounds
towards the end of 1917.

After the war he continued for a while to be more active as
teacher and conductor than as composer. Not until 1923 did he
complete the first two works to make partial and complete use of
the twelve-note method – the Five Pieces for Piano, Op. 23, and
the Suite for Piano, Op. 25. In that same year he also composed his first piece of chamber music since *Pierrot Lunaire,* and
this work, the Serenade, Op. 24, also makes some use of serial
techniques.

In an important letter, dated 1 December 1923, to Josef Matthias
Hauer, the Viennese composer who had also formulated a method
of twelve-note composition, Schoenberg wrote as follows:

My point of departure was the attempt to replace the no longer applicable
principle of tonality by a new principle relevant to the changed conditions:
that is, in theory. I am definitely concerned with no other theories but the
methods of 'twelve-note composition', as – after many errors and deviations –
I now (and I hope definitively) call it. I believe – for the first time again in
fifteen years – that I have found a key. . . . frankly, I have so far – for the first
time – found no mistake and the system keeps on growing of its own accord,
without my doing anything about it. This I consider a good sign. In this way
I find myself positively enabled to compose as freely and fantastically as one
otherwise does only in one's youth, and am nevertheless subject to a precisely
definable aesthetic discipline. It is now more precise than it has ever been. For
I can provide rules for almost everything. [Letter 78]

While not discussing the technical details of the method – in
spite of his use of the word 'system' here, Schoenberg disliked
it – this letter clearly shows the pleasure and relief which the
composer found in having at last developed a positive alternative
to the principle of tonality: an alternative with precise and comprehensive 'rules'. In fact Schoenberg never laid down any rules
for twelve-note composition comparable with his textbooks on
the nature of tonal harmony and counterpoint. What he did was to
define the materials to be used in a twelve-note composition, at a
time when his own music had evolved naturally to a point where
such a definition was possible.

This material consists of a basic set (or row, or series) which presents the twelve chromatic semitones of the chromatic scale in a specific order (cf. Ex. 9, p. 39); the inversion of that set, whereby an ascending major third becomes a descending major third, etc.; the retrogrades of both the basic set and the inversion; and the eleven transpositions of all four, making a total of forty-eight versions. As the analysis of twelve-note music has become more thorough and systematic a simple terminology for identifying these various set-forms has been developed and will be followed below. P-o describes the initial untransposed form of the set – the prime; I-o is the untransposed inversion, R-o the retrograde of P-o, and RI-o the retrograde of I-o. If the basic set is transposed by one semitone (i.e. from C on to C sharp) it becomes P-1; if it is transposed by five semitones (from C on to F) it becomes P-5. These transposition numbers apply to all forty-eight set-forms, so that if P-o and I-o begin on F sharp, P-10 and I-10 will begin on E natural, and so on.

This terminology is useful simply because it makes no attempt to conceal the fact that serial music is to some extent about notes as numbers. Yet neither music nor analysis necessarily becomes arid when terms like RI-8 and P-7 are brought into play. Schoenberg's own attitude to analysis will be discussed more fully later on, yet one point should be made at once. He was most anxious that his works should be considered as 'twelve-note *compositions,* not *twelve-note* compositions' (cf. p. 46). This most certainly does not imply emphasis on the 'composition' to the total exclusion of the 'twelve-note': for it is as pointless to ignore the serial structure of the music in analysis as it is to ignore its traditional, pre-serial aspects. The music is about both features. Analysis of it, even of the most summary kind, should discuss both features too.

The Serenade, Op. 24, for clarinet, bass clarinet, mandoline, guitar, violin, viola, cello and bass voice was begun in September 1921 and finally completed in April 1923. Though a product of the period in which serialism was crystallising, it looks back, in atmosphere and to some extent in form, to the mannerist world of *Pierrot Lunaire.* Nevertheless, its structures are more expansive, and the closely-fashioned thematic developments recall the composer of the D minor Quartet and the First Chamber Symphony. The opening March is a sonata-type movement, with a developmental recapitulation and a main theme which is linked through the last of Berg's Three Orchestral Pieces, Op. 6, to the symphonic marches of Mahler. The finale is a substantial recapitulation of the March, and also includes references to earlier movements, notably the tender Song without Words (no. 6). The seven movements of the work are arranged with some regard for symmetry, as the parallel outer movements suggest. Thus movements two and five (Minuet and Dance-Scene) are both lively and sardonic, while movements three and six (Variations and Song without Words) are more restrained and reflective. The central movement is the only vocal one, a setting of Petrarch's Sonnet 217, and it acts as a focus for both the passionate and the tender qualities of the whole work.

Three movements of the Serenade explore three different types of twelve-note method. In the Sonnet, the vocal part has thirteen statements of the same untransposed twelve-note set (the endings of the vocal phrases only once coinciding with the ending of a statement of a set), while the accompanying instruments freely use the set as a source for motivic material (the final vocal statement is in fact two notes short, the 'missing' pair being provided by the violin and viola). In the first bars of the movement the mandoline and guitar accompany a complete statement of the set (violin, bass clarinet, cello and viola) with chords which avoid doubling the 'melody' notes but which do not themselves derive from that specific ordering of the set which is presented melodically (Ex. 7). Such a relationship – often, at times, tension – between a fixed order and a free arrangement becomes fundamental to Schoenberg's later twelve-note manner, as does his concern to avoid doublings of notes which might tend to create emphases analogous to those in triadic music.

The third movement of the Serenade, Variations, is fourteen-note rather than twelve-note, the theme consisting of a fourteen-note idea and its retrograde, played by the clarinet, unaccompanied. The five variations and coda derive from this material in a manner which recalls the virtually all-thematic texture of the variation movement in the Second String Quartet. This is a movement notable for its contrapuntal flexibility, the various forms of the set being used imitatively as well as harmonically. The way in which the composer derives new shapes from the original set-theme, as in Variation IV, recalls Erwin Stein's useful dictum:

'the repetitions of a row are not the repetitions of a melody';[1] and even when, as in the Sonnet, the melodic character of the music is unmistakable, the intervals of the set perform more than a merely melodic function. Set repetitions affect every dimension of the music, but none more so than the relationship between melody and harmony.

Large sections of the fifth movement of the Serenade (Dance-Scene) make use of two complementary six-note sets, the only 'rule' being that they preserve their own independent pitch content, the actual order of the six notes in each 'half-set' (or hexachord) constantly changing. As has often been pointed out, such 'troping' is similar to Hauer's twelve-note method, and Schoenberg was to find it useful again later on.

The passionate lyricism of the Petrarch setting provides contrast to the at times rather heavy-handed skittishness of the dance movements, the wit of which is most effective when, as in the central sections of the Dance-Scene, Schoenberg seems to be mocking his own atonal dexterity and encouraging the cello to

[1] Stein, *op. cit.,* p. 72.

stress a C sharp. For many listeners, Schoenberg's transference into an atonal, contrapuntal context of forms which depend for their atmosphere on simple textures as well as light moods is his least effective link with tradition. The Mahlerian fixation on a powerful conjunction of grandeur and banality seems in Schoenberg's case to have become a need not merely to inflate simplicity but to mock it, to treat it as if its persistence were an affront to the complex mental processes a composer must perform in order to achieve genuine self-expression in the twentieth century. (It is a syndrome which we see today most notably in the work of Peter Maxwell Davies, where parody is the foundation of savage distortions and dramatic juxtapositions, as in *St Thomas Wake: Foxtrot for Orchestra*, or *Eight Songs for a Mad King*.) In Schoenberg's case, it became increasingly clear as he composed serially that his genius was for reinterpreting the most complex structures of the classical and romantic eras, and he avoided works of the Serenade type. Nevertheless, the actual sound of the music is perfectly imagined in terms of atmosphere. The dreamy sound of the bass clarinet below both the violin melody and the guitar accompaniment at the start of the Song without Words, and the occasional emergence of the delicate mandoline in a thematic role, as at bar 122 of the March, are just two effects which linger in the memory.

It is arguable that free atonality was too negative a concept to satisfy Schoenberg. It was not simply that he needed an 'objective' theory of composition to shield and nurture his subconscious. He needed to feel the kind of working relationship with the music of the past which came about only when some still vital aspect of earlier music was involved. Above all, he sought a means of continuing that technique of developing variation which he felt to be the most progressive feature of the music of Brahms, Mahler and Reger, and which, Schoenberg's own work implies, needs a unity which is both inspired (the totality) and consciously deployed (the details).

It is the Wind Quintet, Op. 26 (1923–4), that shows quite unmistakably Schoenberg's impatience to put twelve-note technique to the test of sustaining fully worked-out classical forms, as well as of demonstrating what he later called 'the unlimited abundance of possibilities' in the forty-eight versions of one single set. The Quintet is one of his most extreme works, and one of the most difficult to perform. It seems to have arisen in part out of an inner conviction that his first completely twelve-note work, the Suite for Piano, Op. 25, was too 'safe', too narrow both in its reliance on eighteenth-century dance forms and in its exclusive exploitation of only eight forms of the basic set – P–o and R–o; P–6 and R–6; I–o and RI–o; I–6 and RI–6. This basic material, with P–o and I–o starting from E and ending on B flat, while P–6 and I–6 start from B flat and end on E, suggests that the composer might have intended analogies with the pivotal tonic and dominant relationships of tonal music. Yet the Suite is certainly not tonally centred on the first note of P–o, and there is little feeling of sets starting on E being used in a primary (tonic) capacity, or of those starting on B flat being used in a subordinate (modulatory) capacity. A sense of hierarchy – of primary and secondary elements – is achieved in a different way.

If the two P and two I sets of Op. 25 are written out and studied with a view to establishing their most striking common features, it soon becomes clear that in each case the third or fourth note is either G or D flat. There is no doubt whatever that Schoenberg turned this important recurring element to compositional account in the work, both melodically and harmonically. On occasion the G and D flat are even alternated in ostinato fashion, and in these places the music almost seems to be tonally centred in the manner of Bartók's more chromatic, less triadic works – for example, his Third String Quartet.

I have taken up space with discussion of a non-chamber work because the Piano Suite demonstrates a vital point about Schoenberg's serialism in a simple, audible way. It may be one of the theoretical axioms of twelve-note technique that, just as all twelve pitches in all forty-eight sets are of equal importance, without the hierarchical emphasis on the first, fifth and fourth degrees found in diatonic scales, so all forty-eight versions of the set are likewise of equal importance. Yet in Schoenberg's practice, stresses of some kind – stresses creating inequality – are normally found, both within the set group as a whole and even within the individual components of that group.

The kind of quasi-tonal emphases detectable in parts of the Piano Suite appears only rarely in the larger multi-movement chamber works, although the use of P–o and I–5 as twin pivots and points of focus in the Third String Quartet has common features with the use of P–o and P–6 in the Suite. Yet Schoenberg did continue the basic principle, established in the Suite, of associ-ating sets with strong similarities in the actual order of their pitches, and at crucial points in the Wind Quintet and the Suite, Op. 29, he even treated the first note of P–o itself as a point of focus within the emphasised group of sets. When all these factors are considered alongside his habit of recapitulating thematic material in the context of sonata, ternary or rondo designs in such a way as to reinforce the theoretical, if not actually audible, primacy of an emphasised set or group of sets, the strong links between tonal and serial procedures in his work become vividly apparent. And in the Wind Quintet a strong sense of hierarchy is fundamental. Not only are tonal forms – sonata, ternary scherzo, ternary slow movement, rondo finale – transplanted, but their tonal basis is translated into serial terms to the extent that P–o and the other three untransposed sets act as the central point of departure and return: and, as will be seen on p. 39, their close relatives are also given significant prominence. In fact, P–o is not just a starting point: it is the nucleus around which everything revolves. Its own constitution also bears witness to tonal modes of thought: the second hexachord is a slightly varied transposition of the first on to the 'dominant'.

It was in the development of polyphonic procedures that Schoenberg found a way of using some of the properties of the twelve-note technique itself, factors which do not arise merely from perceiving analogies with the tonal system – which, after all, twelve-note composition was intended to replace. The opening of the Wind Quintet shows the simplest of these procedures, with the second hexachord of P–o acting as harmonic support to the melo-dic statement of the first hexachord. Like the opening of the Sonnet from the Serenade (Ex. 5, p. 23), this prevents that doubling of notes between melody and harmony which might recall, however briefly, the specific procedures of tonal harmony, and which Schoenberg disliked, possibly because the music had so many other, more subtle, resemblances to tonal music.

Ex. 8

In the Quintet Schoenberg did not apparently take this technique to its next logical step of combining not merely P–o with R–o to achieve a fusion of two distinct hexachords without the same notes appearing twice, but P–o with some other transposition, P or I, which has the same hexachordal content as R–o (in the case of Op. 26 this would be P–7). In many of his later twelve-note works, Schoenberg contrives that P–o and I–5 (and therefore P–1 and I–6, P–2 and I–7, etc.) shall be in a relationship where the first hexachord of one has the same pitches (in different order) as the second of the other. This property, called 'combinatoriality' by the American composer and theorist Milton Babbitt, depends on a recognition of the inevitable relationship between transposition and permutation in any group of forty-eight sets: any transposition of P–o reproduces the same *intervals* in the same order as P–o itself; but at the same time it reproduces the twelve pitches in a *different* order – it is a permutation of P–o as well. Combinatoriality as such is not employed by Schoenberg in the Wind Quintet, though he is obviously concerned to make significant use of sets in which the actual note order is similar. The pitch order of any P–o will naturally be more closely related to that of certain transpositions than to others, and in the case of Op. 26 we can see how the first hexachord (α) of P–o is very similar to the second hexachord (β) of P–5 (five pitches in common,

Ex. 9

and in the same order). It is also close to the first hexachord of I-4 (five pitches in common, though in a different order). The closest link of all is with the second hexachord of I-11, where all six notes are the same, though in a slightly different order; the link with the second hexachord of P-1 is less close simply because the order is so different, though such a distinction would obviously not exist if all the notes of the hexachord were sounded simultaneously.

The 'punning' possibilities between these close relatives are therefore very great, and Schoenberg uses them constantly. In the first movement, for example, the first subject paragraph of the exposition is solely concerned with the four untransposed versions of the basic set. Only in bar 24 (bassoon) is there a change, though the transposition in question, RI-5, is not given prominence at this stage. Its position as a close relative of I-0 is nevertheless clear, and when the second subject paragraph begins, the initial emphasis is on I-4, a transposition closely related to P-0 itself. Schoenberg in fact combines the two relatives (bar 35), and the other new sets introduced later in the exposition – I-11 (bar 50), I-9 (bar 51), P-5 (bar 59) – all have strong common elements. Schoenberg attaches such structural importance to these similarities that it becomes a feature of his serial technique in the Wind Quintet to follow, say, the first hexachord of P-0 with the first of P-7, so that only the last of the twelve notes discloses that the second hexachord of P-0 is not being used. Another type of disguise can be seen in bars 59 and 60 where the composer begins statements of I-9 and P-5 on the fourth pitch, not the first. When he gets to the twelfth pitch he simply continues with the three missing notes – a technique usually known as rotation.

Nowhere is the classical sonata background of this movement clearer than at the end of the exposition, where Schoenberg marks a repeat and composes separate first and second time bars. Yet the importance of not confusing his P-0 with a tonic key or scale in tonal music is marked by the prominence given to that set in the development, as well as to others, like I-5 and P-5, which were also used in the exposition. The development makes the point that in twelve-note music there is a depth of perspective in pitch relationships which enables new aspects of previously exposed material to be explored *within the same basic group of set-*

forms. The more linear and contrapuntal the music, the less opportunity the serial composer has to think in terms of separate and distinct areas defined by chords of substantially different pitch content. One of the weaknesses of the Quintet is, indeed, that it is so persistently polyphonic that even though the composer displays an inexhaustible fund of thematic invention the music is somewhat starved of recognisable harmonic continuity, while the articulating role of rhythm, in the context of an essentially traditional approach to phrase structure, is also inhibited.

Very soon – by the time he had composed his Third String Quartet, Op. 30, in 1927 – Schoenberg was to bring serialism to the point where vertical and horizontal elements were of equal importance. But in the Wind Quintet the constant activity and equality of the individual lines – though not matched by the continual use of five different set-forms in combination – has another result. The music rarely develops an explicitly melodic character: the large-scale classical forms are therefore in some ways merely the sum of a succession of felicitous contrapuntal textures, rather than the background for a dynamic exploration of vertical and horizontal tensions. This is most noticeable in the framing section of the *Poco adagio,* but even in the good-humoured scherzo there is, in places, a plodding quality suggesting that Schoenberg was not yet completely at ease in his new language.

Although it is true that the Wind Quintet does not make out a fully convincing case for serial sonata-form, the finale in particular shows that a coherent development process, in which the identity of a theme remains clear through progressive changes of shape and colour, can be effectively devised. The finale shares with both its predecessor in the Serenade and its successor in the Suite, Op. 29, an element of thematic 'roll-call' in its final stages. This focusing on different thematic shapes, all of which derive from the same basic set, is a kind of parallel to the emphasis on some of the available twelve pitches, an emphasis analogous to 'perspectives' in tonal music, where a given triad may be the tonic of the tonic key, the subdominant of the dominant key, or the dominant of the subdominant key. On those occasions in Op. 26 where Schoenberg sardonically stresses the initial E flat of the entire set-group (cf. the coda to the finale with its 'dominants' and 'tonics' in the bass (bars 326–8) and final unison E flat) one senses behind the feeling of parody an unwillingness to ex-

plore the full potentialities of his own brain-child. As many commentators have noted, Schoenberg never really ceased to compose
against a background not just of tonal forms but also of tonal
harmony, and this in spite of his normal avoidance of octave
doublings. If anything, this is more true of his serial works than
of his 'free' atonal ones: the Wind Quintet is more tonal than the
Serenade. But his greatest serial works are those in which that
tonal background is interpreted through the properties of the
entire twelve-note group – the forty-eight versions of the basic
set – even when P–o is treated, in combination with I–5, as
primus inter pares.

In spite of its ambitiousness, therefore, the Quintet is not a
totally liberating work. Schoenberg launched himself as a mature
composer with *Verklärte Nacht,* a work in which the potential
incompatibility of subject and medium is triumphantly overcome.
As far as Op. 26 is concerned, the choice of a wind quintet certainly ensures maximum clarity for the contrapuntal relationships
so crucial to the work, but the medium is simply not substantial
enough for such elaborate structures, particularly when the texture
is overloaded with thematic references and polyphonic activity.
Certainly it is far less spontaneously melodic than the later
chamber works for strings, and, as we have seen, in the first
movement Schoenberg for once failed to provide a sonata-form
structure with its prime necessity, fully characterised themes –
perhaps the relative lack of interval variety in the set itself accounts
for this. In any case, it seems most unlikely that the Wind Quintet
grew, like Schoenberg's best serial works, from a *melodic* idea
which formed the basis for the twelve-note set. As a whole, therefore, Op. 26 is an impressive and often entertaining achievement,
full of ideas about how serial technique may be explored, but not a
completely satisfying musical experience.

The Wind Quintet was completed in August 1924, and first
performed a few weeks later on 13 September in Vienna, conducted (!) by Felix Greissle. Schoenberg started work on another
bravura chamber composition, the Suite, Op. 29, at the end of
October, but there were various interruptions and the piece was
not finished until May 1926. The first performance, conducted
by the composer, took place in Paris on 15 December 1927.

The Suite is scored for three clarinets (E flat, B flat and bass),
string trio and piano. The brief period between the completion of

the Quintet and the beginning of the Suite may account for the fact that the sets of both works start with the same two pitches. If we reverse the order of the first two notes in the second hexa-chord of the Suite's P–o it becomes an exact transposition of the first, in the relationship R–10. The overall amount of invariance – identity between different transpositions within the set-group – is also increased by the fact that I–5, P–8, P–10 and I–7 are all fairly close relatives of P–o, and Schoenberg's recognition of this is clear, for example, at the start of the fourth movement, a large-scale but still essentially binary Gigue. In the quasi-fugal exposi-tion, P–o and I–5 are at once combined, and I–5 is soon paired with P–8, each hexachord of which has the same pitch content as a hexachord of P–o:

Ex. 10

The next two sets to be introduced, P–10 and I–7, also have strong common links with P–o. It is notable in this intensely imitative context how the piano, when not directly participating in the contrapuntal activity, performs an accompanimental function in which the persistence of certain intervals is the most obvious feature. The two-note harmonic unit of the third or sixth is the most characteristic in the work, and it is heard here not merely as the first interval of the basic set but as a fixed element controlling and giving perspective to the polyphonic superstruc-ture. Thus the very first chords heard in the Suite are not the most typical harmonic sound of the work, simply because they each contain six notes. The set of the Suite is intervallically the least varied Schoenberg ever used in chamber music, and as such provides a relatively primitive solution to the problem of harmonic identity in a serial composition. The stressed third or sixth gives the figuration an almost Brahmsian texture in places, yet although the work is thickly scored at many points the tremendous drive of the music prevents any feeling of stodginess emerging – except, of course, in a dull performance. Witty parodies are again prominent, as in the barely disguised perfect cadence at the end of the first movement. Schoenberg also used a simple E major tune, 'Ännchen von Tharau', as the theme for serial variations in the third movement, with the 'missing' pitches needed to complete each set statement initially provided by a chortling piano accompaniment. Such conjunctions of the banal and the sophisticated are probably best made only in passing, as with 'Ach, du lieber Augustin' in the scherzo of the Second String Quartet, but the movement is not without charm and wit.

Although a dance atmosphere pervades all four movements, the most fundamental weakness of the Wind Quintet – thematic unmemorability – is still not fully conquered. In Schoenberg's greatest music a dazzling capacity for imaginative development is appropriately applied to material strong enough in character to preserve its basic identity. In neither Op. 26 nor Op. 29 is this the case. Only in the Third String Quartet, Op. 30, did he rediscover the soaring lyricism which made the melodies of his tonal music as exciting as his methods of transforming them.

The Suite, Op. 29, is certainly more ambitious in form than the Piano Suite, Op. 25. Simple binary or ternary structures are replaced by elaborate designs which involve considerable emphasis on the introduction of contrasting material as well as on development and recapitulation of the main ideas. Sonata form as such is not used; hence, no doubt, the title, an interesting regression after the ambitious scope of the Wind Quintet: but in its commitment to traditional methods of phrase-building the work is further evidence of the extent to which the exploration of serialism was inseparable in the composer's mind from the reinterpretation of classical compositional devices.

Although the imitative and contrapuntal element is still very prominent in the Suite, the instruments involved ensure that the relatively homogeneous textures of the Quintet are less persistent. The three types of instrument – strings, clarinets and piano – provide much greater opportunities for contrast as well as for combination, and the very opening of the work – staccato chords in wind and strings, broken chords on the piano – is an indication of purely vertical thinking which contrasts strikingly with most of Schoenberg's other openings.

During 1927, the year in which the Third String Quartet was written, Schoenberg taught composition at the Prussian Academy of Arts in Berlin and continued his activities as a conductor. In face of the widespread bewilderment with which even well-disposed music lovers greeted his recent work he must often have reacted as he did in this letter of 12 February 1927:

I usually answer the question why I no longer write as I did at the period of *Verklärte Nacht* by saying: 'I do, but I can't help it if people don't yet recognise the fact.' In the case of some works about which I have been asked this, e.g. my Second String Quartet (incidentally, at the first performance there were the most tremendous scenes I have ever experienced), people are actually beginning to recognise this even now and to forgive me for composing not only as beautifully as before but also very much better than then. But I cannot and of course do not want to blame anyone who is nevertheless not yet capable of feeling complete confidence in it. [Letter 95]

In his 1941 lecture, 'Composition with Twelve Tones', Schoenberg affirmed that the method 'has no other aim than comprehensibility', but he was also convinced that music would develop and remain vital only by being aimed at 'an alert and well-trained mind', a mind which was not content simply with modes of expression which belonged to the past and which had been fully explored by earlier masters.

As far as serial music was concerned, the question quickly arose as to how far an understanding of the details of Schoenberg's procedures was necessary to full appreciation of the musical result. Schoenberg himself was prepared to concede that a knowledge of the pitches and intervals of the basic set was a great help to performers, or at least to singers, to assist in the pitching of difficult passages. Yet he was never completely happy about laying bare the source of his inspiration. Rudolf Kolisch was the leader of the famous string quartet which first performed the Third Quartet on 19 September 1927 in Vienna. Yet no less than five years later we find Schoenberg writing to Kolisch in terms which make it clear that the question, not simply of serial structure, but even of the basic set itself had never arisen before:

You have rightly worked out the series in my string quartet (apart from one detail: the 2nd consequent goes: 6th note C sharp, 7th G sharp). You must have gone to a great deal of trouble, and I don't think I'd have the patience to do it. . . . I can't utter too many warnings against overrating these analyses, since after all they only lead to what I have always been dead against: seeing how it is *done*; whereas I have always helped people to see what it *is*! . . . I can't say it often enough: my works are twelve-note *compositions*, not *twelve-note* compositions. . . . The only sort of analysis there can be any question of for me is one that throws the idea into relief and shows how it is presented and worked out. It goes without saying that in doing this one mustn't overlook artistic subtleties. [Letter 143]

Many later writers have followed Schoenberg in condemning so-called 'analysis' which simply lists in sequence all the transpositions of the set used in a piece, taking no account of the degree to which such transpositions may or may not become audible to the patient listener, nor of the possible relationships of serial structures to traditional musical forms. However, an analysis of a serial work is unlikely to get very far unless it starts with such a 'note-count'. Analysis is, after all, an examination of the process of composition, a means of increasing enjoyment by increasing understanding, on the principle that the more what we hear matches the composer's own creative experience the more satisfying our own experience of the music becomes.

The differences between the sonata-form first movements of the Wind Quintet and the Third String Quartet are immediately striking. In the latter it is clear that Schoenberg is less concerned than formerly with creating a high degree of contrapuntal independence for each part. In the Third Quartet he makes polyphony from the combination of two highly contrasted elements, a textural duality which is mirrored in the emphasis on two sets, though these are not yet fused in the combinatorial relationship defined above. The sets are P–0 and I–5. The textural elements are a vigorous accompanimental *moto perpetuo* and a smooth, lyric melodic line. Technical procedures found in the Wind Quintet and Suite occur here too: for example, Schoenberg exploits the similarity of opening between P–0 and I–9 (G/E and E/G respectively) and also between I–5 and P–8 (C/E flat, E flat/C). The relationship between set choice and sonata structure is simple enough, at least in outline. In the exposition the first subject starts from P–o, the second from I–5: both, though different in character, share a comparable textural duality and explore the same area – that defined by P–o and I–5. In the developmental recapitulation this association is reversed, the inverted second subject coming first and starting from P–o, while the inverted first subject, on its return, starts from I–5. This structural clarity is also enhanced by the characteristic use of *ritenuti* to articulate the sections of the movement.

The tautness of the central development of the first movement is particularly impressive. Both *moto perpetuo* and lyric elements are exploited, and the potential rhythmic monotony of the *moto perpetuo* has already been undermined by skilful displacements of accent at the climax of the first subject paragraph in the exposition: these displacements keep the rhythms alive throughout the movement. The coda contains the widest contrasts of mood and texture, with the *moto perpetuo* silenced at the outset. This passage also shows that the other main function of the coda is to provide concentrated juxtapositions of P–o and I–5, which achieve the ultimate in terseness at the very end, and provide a satisfying sense of harmony crystallising out of melody:

Ex. 11

Only in one sense is that finality deceptive: the P–o/I–5 alternation will be as important in the rest of the work as it has been so far, and even provides, at the end of the second movement, one of Schoenberg's characteristically disguised 'perfect' cadences:

Ex. 12

Having discussed the first movement of the Third Quartet in terms of sonata form it is necessary to admit that, for the composer himself, 'the first and second movements of the third string quartet and the first and last movements of the fourth . . . resemble catalogued forms only in a few respects'.[1] In the absence of other generally accepted criteria, however, I see no reason to abandon Erwin Stein's summary analysis in the published score of the Third Quartet, where the terms exposition, development, recapitulation and coda are all prefaced with the *caveat* 'quasi'. The form of the first movement of the Third Quartet would certainly be unique in Schoenberg if it owed nothing whatever to earlier forms, and I believe that its connection with sonata design is a meaningful one.

As for the second movement, Schoenberg preferred to think of it as a rondo, while once more making it clear that it might not be very useful to try and see the music in terms of conventional forms at all. Several commentators have defined it as a set of variations, or double variations, with rondo characteristics. What is important is not neat pigeon-holing but recognition of the fact that the movement is based on two alternating thematic groups, both lyrical, but the second more diverse in texture, which pass through cumulative stages of variation and development, with a final more recapitulatory section. The actual process of

[1] Cf. Rauchhaupt, *op. cit.,* p. 51.

thematic activity is logical and satisfying, and the form is entirely appropriate to the scope and manner of that activity, even if it 'fails' to conform exactly to the precedents of either variation or rondo as defined in helpful textbooks. In terms of serial technique it is important to remember that thematic variation – the traditional process of reshaping and rearrangement – takes place without a parallel alteration of the twelve-note material itself being implied. The set remains constant: the thematic material deriving from the set is the subject of variation. Yet it is particularly useful with a movement like this, when in danger of being carried away by verbal flights, to recall Hans Keller's stern remark: 'Great structures always mix their formal functions, which is why true analyses of great structures are unreadable.'[1]

A ternary Intermezzo and a sonata-rondo complete the Third String Quartet. In both, elegance and even, on occasion, charm can yield in an instant to those peculiarly Schoenbergian explosions where regular rhythmic patterns and narrow-interval melodic lines are shattered from within. The traditional musical structures are justified because the composer shows that they can still be used in a dramatic, vivid manner.

In the Third Quartet, harmonic identity and thematic identity are more closely integrated than before, not because serial relationships, emotional range and instrumental techniques are simplified but because the texture itself is conceived in terms of shorter and more rigorously contrasted motivic elements which, however, do not hinder the growth of long, flowing, eloquently romantic lines. Schoenberg had now achieved perfect control of the relationship between detail and totality, and although the music is no less 'all-thematic' than that of the Wind Quintet or the Suite its more vividly polarised outlines enable the ear to approach it more confidently. Nevertheless, Schoenberg was not consciously cultivating a harmonic system, analagous to tonality, of different degrees of concord and discord. The increase and decrease of tension is still primarily a rhythmic and textural matter.

After the Third Quartet, once 'combinatoriality' was established as a principle of composition, Schoenberg was naturally no longer concerned with building forms around the relationship between two *separate* sets. Although the polarity of P–o and I–5 in Op. 30

[1] 'Schoenberg as Music', *The Listener,* 7 January 1965, p. 34.

has been stressed here, as it is in the music, it is important to emphasise that, far from being combinatorial in the sense of the first hexachord of each providing the total of twelve notes, his pair of sets has a degree of identity between *similar* hexachords. Like the Second Quartet, then, Op. 30 is technically transitional: and like the Second Quartet, however much we may argue about logic, system and serial properties, it is a masterpiece, one of Schoenberg's greatest works in any medium.

1936 - 1949

Between 1927 and 1936 Schoenberg wrote no chamber music. The major work of this period was the opera *Moses und Aron* – or rather the first two acts of the opera, since he never composed the music for the third. The period also saw the rise to power of the Nazi party in Germany, and in May 1933 Schoenberg left Berlin after the President of the Academy had stated at a Senate meeting that he was obliged to eliminate the 'Jewish influence' in that establishment. His initial destination was France, but finding no prospect of regular employment there he accepted an engagement in Boston, and sailed for America on 25 October 1933. He never returned to Europe.

Schoenberg's first two years in America were far from secure. Only in 1935, when he moved to Hollywood and began to teach at the University of Southern California, did both his health and financial position improve. In 1936, however, he was appointed a professor of music at the University of California, Los Angeles. He moved into the house at Brentwood Park where he was to live until his death in 1951, and soon composed two of his finest works, the Violin Concerto and the Fourth String Quartet.

Although it may be said that Schoenberg was fortunate in escaping to America at a relatively early stage of the Nazi terror, the high degree of disturbance and upheaval involved for a composer in his late fifties whose roots were so strongly embedded in European soil cannot be over-estimated. America was by no means totally congenial: as Schoenberg graphically wrote to Alma Mahler in January 1936: 'Here we are constantly being offered the earth, which then in the end brings forth sour grapes' (Letter 169). The amount of teaching expected of him, with the resulting difficulty in finding time to compose, was another problem, as this letter to Mrs Elizabeth Sprague Coolidge, who commissioned the Fourth String Quartet, shows:

I finished the quartet on July 26 [1936] and should have sent it to you if only I knew where you are now.... You were probably astonished to hear nothing more from us. But you could not imagine how much work we had through the arrival of our furniture. I lost more than four weeks and still have my library and my manuscripts not arranged. Besides I had to teach. Private lessons and these terrible summer sessions at USC. But every quarter of an hour I was free I used for the continuation of the string quartet. When you will get the manuscript you will see the first three movements were finished in a rather short time. But the fourth movement which I began on June 18 took more time than the other three. But not for composing. I am very content with the work and think it will be much more pleasant than the third. But – I always believe so. [Letter 173]

Even allowing for Schoenberg's inexperience of the English language, 'pleasant' seems an extraordinary word to apply to any of his works, but especially the powerful and passionate Fourth Quartet. The first movement was actually begun on 27 April 1936 and finished on 12 June; Schoenberg worked on the second movement from 24 May to 10 June, and finished the third on 18 June. Then, as his letter explains, the finale was written between 18 June and 26 July. A note on the score at bar 22 of the first movement was made on 9 May, when moving house caused a ten-day interruption. Schoenberg was also 'stuck for a day' at bar 206 in the later stages of the first movement, though the continuity of the music is unaffected.[1]

Following the series of concerts in which the Quartet was given its first performance, Schoenberg again wrote to Mrs Coolidge, saying how marvellously the Kolisch Quartet had played, but complaining about the lack of congratulations offered to him by university officials:

You have certainly already realised that I am not ambitious and I do not expect people to understand my music at the first hearing. I am content if they do not dislike it when they hear it the fifteenth time. [Letter 174]

It seemed that, after all, Los Angeles in the 1930s was no different from Vienna in the 1900s. Today the Fourth Quartet is one of the most familiar of Schoenberg's twelve-note works, and the one which has been most fully discussed and most frequently played.

[1] Details from Rufer, *op. cit.,* p. 62.

It is the last of Schoenberg's works for the medium, though sketches for a fifth were found among his papers, and it is the last of his chamber works to preserve the 'classic' order of four separate movements, confirming that the composer's aim was not to develop totally new forms appropriate to a new composition technique, but to discover common ground between the new technique and the old forms. The very expansiveness of its structures and moods indicates at once why the Fourth Quartet is often felt to be the most approachable of the composer's serial pieces and also why, after finishing it and its companion the Violin Concerto in the same year, he began once more to use single-movement designs. The greatest achievements of Schoenberg's youth and old age, at least as far as chamber music is concerned, were single-movement works. In the case of the First String Quartet, Op. 7, as we have seen, the creation of one movement from elements of fast first movement, scherzo and slow movement enable Schoenberg to avoid, by compression, the need for substantial periods of recapitulation and to undermine the tonally orientated harmonic direction which such works had traditionally demanded. When in the twelve-note works he confirmed his readoption (in the Second Quartet) of the separate-movement sonata, he used the need for recapitulation as a means of justifying his emphasis on one particular combined pair of sets (P–o and I–5) and on one particular melodic idea which had, in all probability, been the source of the set itself.

In the last three chamber works, however, Schoenberg arrived at forms in which the classical structural divisions and the traditional melodic identities of much of his earlier music are both set aside. And even in the first movement of the Fourth Quartet the 'separation' of sonata form into exposition, development and recapitulation is far from clear. The movement conforms to the extent that a melodic idea, stated at the outset, dominates the music by its pitch, rhythm and general shape, but the other elements appropriate to traditional sonata form are less neatly observable than in the corresponding movement of the Third Quartet, composed nearly ten years earlier.

In the Fourth Quartet Schoenberg was still revelling in the freedom which serial technique gave him to set up numerous associations with the music of the past and yet to retain his own identity. The main associations derive from the clearly identifiable melodic lines, with their accompanying harmonies and figurations; from a cadence-directed phrase structure; from imitative counterpoint; and from the occasional sense (at least in the outer movements) of an emphasis on the first pitch of P–o (D) which gives it the function of a pitch centre – though *not* of a tonality. As is often the case with Schoenberg, it is easier to describe the music in terms of its modifications of classical form than in terms of its reinterpretations of them in the light of the properties of serialism itself. In the first movement, for example, a note-count establishes that Schoenberg uses all twelve pairs of sets at least once, a P or R form always relating to the I or RI form five semitones above it. But at the points where, in tonal music, a modulation would most normally occur, like the 'second subject' in the exposition, he does not necessarily change the pair of sets in use.

This reinforces the necessity of not identifying a set with a key or scale, or a change of set with a modulation. It may eventually be possible to explain why Schoenberg moved from one particular set to another at a given point, independent of considerations of classical form, but, at least in the case of the Fourth String Quartet, such 'reasons' are certainly not immediately apparent. Without getting involved in the arguments put forward by George Perle and others, which assert that Schoenberg's concern with tonal analogies prevented him from fully exploring the properties of serialism itself, it seems clear that these analogies could have been carried much farther had Schoenberg so desired.

One way in which Schoenberg continued to exploit the serial relationships themselves, as distinct from their melodic or harmonic results, is in the capacity for punning between two sets which have similar pitch arrangements. Thus the second phrase of the ternary second movement begins in a manner similar to the first, but a note-count shows that the set involved is not P–o but R–3 (see Ex. 13 overleaf).

Serial relationships also play a part in organising the binary structure of the third movement. The first half begins with P–10 and quickly proceeds to its complement I–3. The second half reverses the process. The melody in question, played by all four instruments in unison, is passionately eloquent or emptily rhetorical according to taste. The repetitions, rhythms and dynamics are certainly not typical of the composer. They almost

Ex. 13

suggest half-hearted auditioning for Hollywood – but this is only so when taken out of context. The movement as a whole is full of subtle unpredictabilities (e.g. bars 622–9), as well as moments of almost affectionate academicism (cf. the fugato, bars 671 ff).

As far as the development processes of the first movement are concerned, however, it is important to clarify some of the possibilities inherent in the method which the composer employs. The fact that the main theme, in its initial form, uses all twelve notes of P–0 in the correct order sets a precedent, and just as tonal developments present versions of the exposition material in different tonalities, so Schoenberg develops his theme by showing how different transpositions of the set can yield different versions of that theme, depending entirely on which pitches are thematic and which accompaniment. At one point, by contrast, two different transpositions yield the *same* version of a motive deriving from the first subject. In bars 153–4 the viola has notes 1, 2, 3, 8, 9 and 10 of P–1 – E flat, D, B flat, C sharp, A, G sharp (note the sequential effect): then in bars 155–6 the first violin has notes 3, 4, 5, 10, 11 and 12 of RI–6: the pitches and rhythms are the same as the viola's.

Development is a matter of choice – not just of choosing which set-pair should follow which, but of choosing how similar or how remote from the original layout the particular statement should be. Another source of variation is in the relationship between the hexachords of the set-pairs, whereby the P and I elements may either be combined or stated consecutively. At the start of the first movement P–o and I–5 are not stated in combination until bar 27, while at bar 200 the arrangement whereby the top two parts carry one hexachord of the P or I form and the bottom parts carry the complement is changed; the outer parts have one form, the inner parts the other. The whole movement is proof of the rich variety which an imaginative composer can draw from the combinatorial principle. It is the reverse of rigid, the antithesis of mathematical.

The finale, which begins by contrasting *amabile* and *agitato* elements, is particularly rich in contrapuntal activity, and in the combination of *cantabile* and fragmented lines (cf. notably bars 831 ff). The coda provides clinching juxtapositions of the P–o/I–5 relationship. Schoenberg stresses the D from the retrograde of the latter set in bar 929, and the final cadence is virtually a disguised plagal on D which dissolves in the last bars to end on a rather hesitant semicolon.

Ex. 14

(end of 4th movt.)

poco rit.

The Fourth String Quartet is no more concerned than any other work of Schoenberg's with instrumental effect for its own sake, but its use of the medium, especially in the second movement, is distinctively imaginative and wide-ranging. Schoenberg did not invent one particular device as easily recognisable, or as easily abused, as Bartók's 'snap' pizzicato, but he is the equal of the more popular composer in his resourcefulness and his ability to make effect the servant rather than the master of musical argument.

Between the composition of the Fourth Quartet and his next chamber work, the *Ode to Napoleon,* Op. 41 (1942), Schoenberg penned an even more decisive letter on the subject of twelve-note analysis than the one to Kolisch of 1932 (see p. 46), probably as the result of his belief that in America young people were

extremely good at getting hold of principles, but then want to apply them too much 'on principle'. And in art that's wrong. What distinguishes art from science

is: that here there should not be principles of the kind one has to use on principle: that the one 'narrowly' defines what must be left 'wide open' [in the
other?]; that musical logic does not answer to 'if –, then –', but enjoys making
use of the possibilities excluded by 'if –, then –'. [Letter 183]

In May 1938 Schoenberg had written to Arthur Locke as
follows:

Now one word about your intention to analyse these pieces as regards to the
use of the basic set of twelve tones. I have to tell you frankly: I could not do
this. It would mean that I myself had to work days to find out, how the twelve
tones have been used and there are enough places where it will be almost
impossible to find the solution. I myself consider this question as unimportant
and have always told my pupils the same.[1]

The *Ode to Napoleon* might almost have been written to illustrate
Schoenberg's apparent belief that twelve-note counting was
futile, since one of the initial principles of serialism – that the
twelve-note set derives from a certain ordering of the twelve
chromatic semitones which is retained throughout the composition in question – is here persistently set aside. Yet what is most
interesting about Schoenberg's admission in the above letter is
not his dislike of note counting. It is his statement that he would
not immediately himself be able to recall which set was involved
at any given point: more evidence, if it were needed, of the fact
that Schoenberg still composed instinctively, if 'methodically'.
Whereas, before the *Ode*, the set had been used in a particular
pitch-order often enough for its identity to be clear, however
many incidental deviations there may have been from that order,
in Op. 41 the character of the music derives from interval relationships which can emerge whatever order of notes is used.

The *Ode* exists in two versions: Op. 41(a) for reciter, piano
and string quartet, and Op. 41(b) with string orchestra replacing
the quartet. Byron's extended and bitter attack on Napoleon was
clearly relevant to the would-be dictators of the Second World
War, and Schoenberg's music matches it to perfection, not merely
in mood but also in technique. The musical reference to Beethoven's Fifth Symphony at the line 'the earthquake voice of
Victory' is itself evidence of Schoenberg's ironic intention.
He was not simply writing a sermon on the evils of overweening
ambition, any more than Byron was. The *Ode* is a bitter analysis of
human weakness, and in this sense the occasional triadic references

[1] Rufer, *op. cit.,* p. 141.

and the pseudo-tonal ending become ironic rather than, in any sense, affirmative. The heroic 'Eroica' key of E flat is used to mock all human pretentiousness. Nor is the *Ode* a hymn to man's adaptability, his ability to survive the trials of repression: such a work would be altogether calmer and more noble than Schoenberg's white-hot tirade.

Appropriately, when the deep disruptiveness of all evil is the main subject, serial technique itself becomes literally disordered, until it resembles that of the other pioneer of twelve-note music, Josef Matthias Hauer. Hauer divided the twelve chromatic semitones into two groups of six, and within each hexachord the pitches could appear in any order. A thorough-going exploitation of this technique could ensure that there were no recurrences of identical thematic statements at all. Yet Schoenberg retains thematic identity, and the large-scale single-movement form of the *Ode* is unified in no small part by a recurrent idea which 'orders' the original hexachord:

Ex. 15

In a letter to René Leibowitz, dated 4 July 1947, Schoenberg wrote:

it is true that the Ode at the end sounds like E flat. I don't know why I did it. Maybe I was wrong, but at present you cannot make me feel this. [Letter 216]

He may have done it in part out of his belief, referred to in the same letter, that there were 'many unused possibilities' in the gap between his tonal and serial works – a gap which he himself had explored in the Second Chamber Symphony, the Variations on a Recitative for organ, and other works of the 1930s and 1940s. He can hardly have seen, in the no-man's-land between the triad and strict twelve-note procedures, a powerful symbol of extremism. The symbol, if it exists, is one of chaos, which can be as much the product of ill-conceived compromise as of unremitting extremism. In any case, the *Ode* cannot have been written as the result of long, philosophical speculation. It is a deeply personal expression of bitterness, in which anger and nostalgia, far from neutralising each other, combine to produce one of the composer's most direct statements. The use of heightened speech, notated on, above or below a single line which represents the normal pitch level of the reciter's speaking voice, inevitably makes it difficult at times to hear important details of the instrumental argument, but the manner is as appropriate to the often hectoring quality of Byron's words as are the swooping contours of the *Sprechgesang* in *Pierrot Lunaire* and the tortured arches of Moses' part in *Moses und Aron*.

Schoenberg made his own attitude clear in a letter of 15 January 1948 to his pupil and biographer H. H. Stuckenschmidt:

Lord Byron, who had at first admired Napoleon greatly, was so disappointed by his simple resignation that he made him the object of his bitterest scorn. I do not think that I failed to reflect this in my composition.[1]

This comment warns us against pursuing any analogy between Napoleon and Hitler, relevant though many of the details of the poem are to any situation in which an arrogant dictator takes on more than he can control or conquer. Byron's attitude to Napoleon was different from Schoenberg's view of Hitler, and it is the final product of the *Ode*'s ironic intensity that the Narrator himself, the voice of the poet, should seem to take on the very attributes of the person and the type which he condemns so eloquently. The Narrator of the *Ode* is not himself the protagonist: he is simply, like every person fascinated by a corrupt dictator, himself liable to become corrupt. The more savage the criticism, the more envious the critic.

The serial technique of the *Ode* looks back, as George Perle has pointed out,[2] to that of Schoenberg's earliest experiments in this style, particularly those in the Serenade, Op. 24. In the same year, however, he composed the Piano Concerto, Op. 42, which, although resembling the *Ode* to the extent of being in one movement and in having occasional tonal tendencies, is not very different from the Fourth String Quartet or the Violin Concerto in basic texture and phraseology. Clear distinctions obtain between melodic lines and supporting harmonies, and there is an equally clear distinction between the four sections of the one movement,

---

[1] Rufer, *op. cit.*, p. 69.
[2] *Serial Composition and Atonality* (2nd ed., London 1969), p. 93.

although the finale section contains a recapitulation of the opening idea of the whole work at its original pitch. In very few senses is the Concerto a preparation for the composer's next major work, the String Trio, Op. 45 (1946). The concentration, discontinuity and violence of the Trio, though not implying an absence of unity, of expressiveness, even at times of nostalgia, are remarkable, occurring as they do with such spontaneity and originality in the work of a man of seventy-one who, the previous year, had suffered the humiliation of having his application for a Guggenheim Foundation Grant – which would have enabled him to give up teaching and concentrate entirely on composition – rejected. On 2 August 1946 Schoenberg suffered a collapse, his heartbeat being restored only by a timely injection. Yet on the 20th of the same month he began the Trio and completed it only five weeks later, on 23 September.

The Trio, as Schoenberg told Thomas Mann, was in some ways a musical reflection of the physical and psychological impact of that severe illness. The tough, uncompromising emphasis on abrupt contrasts, and the frequent use of expressionistic string effects (*ponticello, col legno,* harmonics, tremolos) might seem to represent an almost frantic attempt on Schoenberg's part to demonstrate that his creative vitality was unimpaired after his near-death. The most impressive quality of the Trio, nevertheless, is not the sheer range of diverse elements, but their control – the creation of a coherent single-movement structure remote in many ways from that of earlier works like the D minor Quartet, Op. 7, or the First Chamber Symphony, Op. 9 – and the completely convincing integration of violence and expressiveness, culminating in a tender, valedictory coda which is arguably Schoenberg's most beautiful after Op. 7.

The single movement of the Trio divides into five sections: three 'Parts' (although the first is not so described in the score – probably a simple omission by Schoenberg) separated by two Episodes. Devotees of Bartók will recognise the possibilities for arch form (ABCBA) which such a scheme offers – or, at any rate, for some kind of rondo-derivative. However, Schoenberg is not concerned with the sort of symmetry which Bartók exploits so effectively in his Fourth and Fifth String Quartets. The structural outline of the Trio may show strong traditional features relatable, for example, to *Verklärte Nacht,* but the details are strikingly original. Melodic identity matters much less here than in all the previous twelve-note chamber works, and in several places even the classical antecedent/consequent phrase structure, still operative in the *Ode to Napoleon* and the Piano Concerto, gives way to an apposition of short, contrasted units in which the identity and continuity of traditional musical discourse are replaced by gestures of almost subliminal brevity.

Part One acts as a wild introduction in which obviously thematic, melodic ideas are less important than dramatic chordal outbursts and arpeggios. The first Episode opens with a strong contrast – a sustained lyric statement. This is brushed aside by more explosions, but the essentially lyric character of the section is affirmed in a more extended passage in which all three instruments share in the statement of melodic material (bars 86 ff). Another disruption, and the first Episode ends with one of the most regular melodic sections of the whole work (bars 122 ff). It is the mysterious effect of passages like this, not to make the wilder moments seem in some sense improvisatory, but to make audible ways in which both types of material derive from the same roots, the same set-group.

Part Two starts with two attempts to continue the lyrical manner, both of which are disrupted. Only in bar 159 does an extended melodic paragraph begin to unfold (the idea will return, inverted, in the coda to the whole work). After ten bars this too ceases. Part Two ends quietly, with wisps of melody and the rarely absent reiterated chords.

The second Episode begins violently and in spite of some brief lyric phrases remains essentially disruptive. Part Three begins like Part One and recapitulates aspects of the whole work. There is no attempt to transform earlier material to achieve a more integrated mood, and the coda (bars 282–93) concludes the work in an atmosphere removed as far as possible from the turmoil of the beginning, a characteristically Schoenbergian ending compounded of diffidence and tenderness (Ex. 16).

Several important general conclusions about the String Trio may emerge from this short description. Recapitulation (more or less transformed) remains as vital a feature as in Schoenberg's more conventionally structured chamber works. What is recapitulated is, however, not the necessarily extended melodic paragraphs of relatively regular phrase structure. These are intermingled with

Ex. 16

the more fragmented, concentrated statements which have done so much to give the work its forceful character. What has changed is nothing less than the concept of *exposition*. As long as he continued to compose against a background of sonata and other traditional forms, Schoenberg could with justification retain a distinction between an exposition of melodic ideas and sections comparable to the classical development and recapitulation (notably in the first movement of the Third String Quartet). In the Trio, however, he seems to have reacted against this concept, possibly out of recognition of the fact that a twelve-note set can be just as validly used to provide continuously changing thematic statements as it can to develop *existing* statements. Since twelve-note music is, by definition, total variation, one can either start with a main thematic idea, as was Schoenberg's own normal practice, and base the movement on that: or one can use the set itself as the source of a whole succession of statements which, by strategic repetition and variation, unify the diverse elements of the form.

In view of the preoccupation of many more recent composers with 'mosaic' structures and various types of musical collage it is not surprising that Schoenberg's String Trio should seem a great step forward, an astonishing development for an ailing composer of seventy-two. In Op. 45, undoubtedly, unity is still partly the result of thematic identity, hence the summarising function of Part Three. Yet the most persistent identity is unmistakably that of the set itself. At times Schoenberg exploits purely serial variety by reordering the hexachords of the set, and using each reordering for long enough to establish a new identity. Nevertheless, there is no suggestion of the complete freedom of note order found in the *Ode to Napoleon,* and the paired use of P–o and I–5, as in earlier works, enables the composer to exploit the tension between their ordered independence and their un-ordered identity. After all, if the first hexachord of P–o and the second of I–5 are sounded as six-note chords, they are indistinguishable. Only melodic statements of the two can display the full extent of their dissimilarity.

The most far-reaching result of Schoenberg's new-found independence of melodic exposition is, then, his escape from the tendency to let emphasis on a particular pitch arrangement of the set become audible, or tend, however nebulously, to create a pitch centre (e.g. the D of the Fourth Quartet, the E flat of the Wind Quintet and the Suite, Op. 29). Perhaps the triads of the *Ode* and other works of the period exorcised this. Or more likely the conflation of exposition and development into one dramatic, evolutionary complex revealed dynamic possibilities in serialism itself which Schoenberg's deep concern with the preservation of aspects of earlier music had helped to obscure.

The last of Schoenberg's chamber compositions, the Phantasy for violin with piano accompaniment, Op. 47, was composed in 1949 and first performed in Los Angeles in September of that year at the composer's seventy-fifth birthday concert by the dedi-

catee, Adolf Koldofsky. As Rufer has shown from his examination
of the original manuscript, the complete violin part was composed
first (between 3 and 22 March), the complementary set-forms for
use in the piano part being indicated but not worked out musically.[1]
The Phantasy marks a further stage in Schoenberg's advance from
classically based forms, though it has structural features in common with the String Trio and even, in a general sense, with the
First Chamber Symphony. Thus the first of the five main sections
(bars 1–33) forms the basis of the final section (bars 154–66): yet
this highly concentrated recapitulation contains no references to
other sections of the work, and the three central sections act as
individually characterised episodes which succeed each other
without cross-references of the melodic/thematic type, creating,
in sum, a totally satisfying balance. Here, as in the Trio, exposition
and development have coalesced to the extent that each episode
except the last exposes new material while exploiting various areas
of the set-group. Schoenberg still distinguishes between primary
(thematic) and subordinate (accompaniment) material – the
music remains remote from the sort of exclusive reliance on small
motivic groups normally found in Webern. By 1945, however,
it is clear that the need to place serial compositions against a
background of tonal forms had passed. A set-group itself could
provide the background for a satisfactory structure, even if, as
David Lewin implies, the way it does so in the Violin Phantasy is
not unlike the tonal process of modulation from one 'region' of
basic tonality to another.[2] Clearly, however, it is the set itself
which provides unity and continuity, not the thematic ideas which
determine it, or derive from it. Schoenberg himself never abandoned his preference for hierarchies within the set-group: the
last twenty-three bars of Op. 47 return to the initial P–0/I–5
relationship. Nor did his new-found delight in the large-scale
integration of extreme contrasts inhibit his melodic inspiration:
the soaring *lento* line (bars 40–51) from the work's second section
proves that:

---

[1] Rufer, *op. cit.*, p. 74.
[2] B. Boretz and E. T. Cone (eds), *Perspectives on Schoenberg and Stravinsky*
(Princeton 1968), pp. 78–92.

Ex. 17

A strong sense of classical types of phrase structure remains to shape the rhythmic diversity of the piece, and to reinforce the conviction that, far from rejecting the past in his old age, Schoenberg had simply reached a new understanding of, a new relationship with, the traditions by which he set such store.

In an article called 'National Music' Schoenberg wrote:

My teachers were, in the first place, Bach and Mozart; in the second place, Beethoven, Brahms and Wagner.

[After detailing precisely what he had learned from these masters, he goes on:]

also learned much from Schubert as well as from Mahler, Strauss and Reger. I closed my mind against no one and could, therefore, say of myself:

My originality comes from the fact that I immediately imitated everything good that I ever saw. Even if I did not see it first in the works of others.

And I may say this: often enough, I saw it first in my own work. For I did not merely stick to what I had seen; I took it over in order to possess it, and it led to something new.

I am convinced that, one day, it will be recognised how closely this 'something new' is related to the best models of the past that have been given us. I lay claim to the merit of having written really new music which, as it rests on tradition, is destined to become a tradition.[1]

Forty years after that claim was made, and more than twenty years after Schoenberg's death, we can demonstrate and accept the traditional foundation of his original achievement. We can also observe that it is an achievement on which others are building, from which others are learning. Schoenberg has in truth become a tradition, but a tradition as alive to those who admire his music as the work of his own 'teachers' always remained to him.

[1]Rufer, *op. cit.*, pp. 147–8.